KEYSTONE TOMBSTONES

BIOGRAPHIES OF FAMOUS PEOPLE BURIED IN PENNSYLVANIA

VOLUME TWO

JOE FARRELL AND JOE FARLEY

SUNBURY
PRESS
Mechanicsburg, PA USA

Published by Sunbury Press, Inc.
Mechanicsburg, Pennsylvania

SUNBURY
P R E S S
www.sunburypress.com

For information about special discounts for bulk purchases, please contact Sunbury Press
Orders Dept. at (855) 338-8359 or orders@sunburypress.com.

To request one of our authors for speaking engagements or book signings, please contact
Sunbury Press Publicity Dept. at publicity@sunburypress.com.

SECOND SUNBURY PRESS EDITION: February 2020

Set in Adobe Garamond. Interior design by Crystal Devine | Cover by Lawrence Knorr.
Edited by Lawrence Knorr and the authors.

Publisher's Cataloging-in-Publication Data
Names: Farrell, Joe, author | Farley, Joe, author.
Title: Keystone tombstones volume two : biographies of famous people buried in pennsylvania
/ Joe Farrell and Joe Farley.
Description: Revised trade paperback edition. | Mechanicsburg, PA : Sunbury Press, 2020. |
Includes biographical references and index.
Summary: Joe farrell and joe farley write about famous and infamous people buried in
pennsylvania after visiting their graves.
Identifiers: ISBN 978-1-62006-293-7 (softcover).
Subjects: BISAC: BIOGRAPHY & AUTOBIOGRAPHY / Rich & Famous. | HISTORY /
US History / Mid-Atlantic.

Product of the United States of America
0 1 1 2 3 5 8 13 21 34 55

Continue the Enlightenment!

And, when he shall die,
Take him and cut him out in little stars,
And he will make the face of Heaven so fine
That all the world will be in love with night
And pay no worship to the garish sun.

—William Shakespeare

Contents

Acknowledgments

The success of *Keystone Tombstones Volume One* has led to this volume. We would like to thank all of those who purchased our first book and encouraged us to continue this series.

Our work has been well-received and supported by many in the media. We especially want to thank Brian Lockman, Francine Schertzer, Corinna Wilson and Alanna Koll as well as the whole crew at the Pennsylvania Cable Network for their tremendous support and interest in Keystone Tombstones. We are also grateful to Mike Rozansky and Tirdad Derakhshani of the *Philadelphia Inquirer* and Brian O'Neill of the *Pittsburgh Post Gazette* for bringing our book to the attention of readers at both ends of the state. We extend special thanks to Stacy Smith, Jill Neely, Kristine Sorenson and John Burnett for having us on Pittsburgh Today Live not once but twice. We deeply appreciate it.

We'd like to thank David Dunkle of the *Harrisburg Patriot News* for being the first to write about Keystone Tombstones. Other reporters to whom we would like to extend our appreciation to James McClure of the York Daily Record, Jack Brubaker of the *Lancaster Intelligencer Journal*, Jim Dino from the *Hazleton Standard-Speaker* and Peter Durantine of "The Burg."

We are also grateful to Betsy Benson, Julie Talerico and Kristofer Collins of *Pittsburgh Magazine* and Jen Merrill and Patti Boccassini of *Harrisburg Magazine* for their reports on our adventures.

In Central Pennsylvania we'd like to extend our thanks to Megan Lello and Scott Lamar at WITF and Chuck Rhodes at WTPA-TV for their interest and support of our project.

A number of bookstores took a particular interest in *Volume One* and we are grateful to Debbie Beamer at the Mechanicsburg Mystery Bookshop, Dani Weller at the Harrisburg Mid Town Scholar, and Ann

Barnett at the State Museum Bookstore. In addition we'd like to thank Kristi Fisher and Donna Wench at the Barnes and Noble Bookstores in Camp Hill and Wilkes Barre respectively. John Hopkins at Christ Church Preservation Trust and Anna Hiner at Westminster Presbyterian Church were particularly helpful.

We'd like to thank Bill Isler for his assistance and many contributions to this volume as well as *Volume One*. We'd be remiss if we didn't thank Rex Fleetwood and Maureen Coyle of the Philadelphia Pyramid Club for their hospitality. We'd also like to thank Larry Brown for being Larry Brown.

Once again we thank Jim Farley for his typing assistance and Julie Dougherty for her interest and technical support as well as Lawrence and Tammi Knorr of Sunbury Press for their continued support.

Lastly we thank Sharon Farley and Mary Wigdahl for their emotional support and their promotional efforts throughout both volumes. If it weren't for them, we'd probably be drinking in some bar on the Lincoln Highway.

Introduction

When we first began this undertaking, our idea was to write a single book. However, as we began working on the project, we realized it wasn't going to be possible. Based on our research, we knew we had enough information to do multiple volumes. Also, friends and other people had gotten in touch with us, suggesting people that deserve to be included in the series. This book marks the second volume, and there will certainly be more to follow.

Armed with a lengthy list of names to consider for inclusion in *Volume Two*, we sat down at Nick's Café in New Cumberland, Pennsylvania, for our initial meeting. By the time we finished, we had decided on thirty potential chapters for this volume. As time went on, we reduced the number to twenty-seven. This volume includes chapters on Pennsylvania businessmen, pioneers, entertainers, founding fathers, murderers, war heroes, sports stars, martyrs of the labor movement, and victims of a natural disaster. We hope that you enjoy reading about all of them.

We split up the chapters evenly and began making trips to photograph the gravesites and other monuments that related to the stories we were trying to tell. Based on our previous experience, we had a much easier time getting around the cemeteries on this go-round. Once again, we were taken by how well some of the cemeteries are cared for while others, unfortunately, are neglected. We urge those responsible to take care of these historic sites.

We used the same plan in writing this volume, as we did in our first book. Once either of us finished a chapter, it was given to the other author for his review and comments. Based on the feedback we received, we would then revise the chapter. The book is the result of shared labor. Another similarity between this book and *Volume One* is the "If You Go" section that concludes each chapter. Here we tell you about other graves you may want to visit, and we also suggest places in the area where you might want to stop for refreshments. Once again, we received no compensation from any of the businesses mentioned in this section.

We continue to visit as many Medal of Honor recipients as possible. This volume contains a chapter on those heroes, and we have included pictures of their gravesites. Also, we have a section that includes photos of unusual graves that we came across on our journeys.

We would be remiss if we didn't thank all of you who purchased *Volume One*. We believe that volume proved to be a success. We have appeared on television shows in Pittsburgh and Harrisburg and will be appearing in Philadelphia in November 2012. Also, we have filmed a series based on *Volume One* that will be shown on the Pennsylvania Cable Network beginning this fall. We can only hope that this volume meets with similar success.

So, there you have it. We believe that this book has something for everyone. We certainly learned a lot in putting it together. We think it includes some great stories that most people will be reading for the first time. Once again, we urge you to visit some of the sites identified in this volume. Many are more than worth a visit.

I.

DON RICHARD "RICHIE" ASHBURN

"His Whiteness"

County: Montgomery • Town: Gladwyne
Buried at Gladwyne United Methodist Church Cemetery
316 Righters Mill Road

The 1950s has long been considered part of the "Golden Age of Baseball." There is little doubt that the glamour position during that decade was centerfield. Three centerfielders, all of whom played for teams who made their home in New York City, dominated the attention of baseball fans around the country. Mickey Mantle, Willie Mays, and Duke Snider were all prolific sluggers, and of course, baseball fans love the long ball. Songs have been written about the trio, and to this day, their fans still argue over who was better. While all this was going on, another centerfielder was plying his trade in a city just down the road. By the end of the '50s, no major leaguer had banged out more base hits during that decade than this Philadelphia Phillie. His name was Richie Ashburn.

The future Hall of Famer was born on a farm in Tilden, Nebraska, on March 19, 1927. His father operated the largest general store in the area. Among his childhood friends was a young man by the name of Johnny Carson, who would go on to make quite a name for himself as an entertainer. Ashburn was drawn to the national pastime and played for the American Legion as well as Tilden High School. In 1944 he was selected to represent Nebraska in the prestigious *Esquire* All-American Boys Baseball game held in New York City. It was there his talents began to draw the attention of major league scouts.

The Philadelphia Phillies signed Ashburn in 1945. He made that team's major league roster in 1948 when he was 21. In his rookie year, he showcased the abilities that would mark his career hitting .333 with an

Don Richard "Richie" Ashburn

on-base percentage of .410 and stealing 32 bases in 117 games. Many felt that Ashburn deserved National League Rookie of the Year honors, but the award went to Alvin Dark.

The 1950 Phillies team was nicknamed the "Whiz Kids" because the average age of the team was 26.4 years. This young team played consistent baseball throughout the season, and by September 20th, they found themselves in first place with a 7 1/2 game lead over Boston and a nine-game lead over Brooklyn. It was at this point in the season that injuries began to take their toll, and the losses mounted. On the last day of the season, the Phils held a one-game lead over the team they would play to finish the year, the Brooklyn Dodgers.

The Phillies started their pitching ace, Robin Roberts, in the season finale, and the Dodgers sent Don Newcombe to the mound. Both men pitched extremely well, and after eight innings, the score was tied at 1–1. In the last of the 9th, Roberts walked Cal Abrams, and he moved to second on a single by Pee Wee Reese. Duke Snider hit a hard single to center that was fielded by Ashburn. Abrams attempted to score, but a perfect throw from Ashburn nailed him at the plate. Roberts then retired the side, and the game went into extra innings. The Phillies opened the top of the 10th with consecutive singles, putting men on first and second with Ashburn coming to the plate. He laid down a sacrifice bunt that advanced the runners to second and third. Dick Sisler followed with a three-run homer that provided the margin of victory as the Phillies won their first pennant since 1915.

The "Whiz Kids" faced the heavily favored New York Yankees in the World Series. Three of the four games were decided by one run, but the Phillies lost all three contests. The Yankees completed the sweep by winning game four by a score of 5–2. Philadelphia only managed three earned runs in the series, one of which was driven in by Ashburn. While many thought this would be the first of many post-game appearances for the Phillies, it would be the first and last World Series for Ashburn. The Phillie centerfielder was quite candid in his opinion as to why this young team failed to repeat: "We were the last to get any black players. We were still pretty good, but they were just getting better." Considering Ashburn's opinion, it is worth remembering that the 1950 World Series was the last in baseball history to match two all-white teams.

While postseason honors may have eluded Ashburn, he continued to perform during the regular season. He had a fifteen-year major league career that included twelve years playing for the Phillies. He was among the most consistent leadoff hitters in major league history and was a terrific centerfielder. Ashburn won the National League batting title twice first in 1955 and again in 1958. In three other years, his batting average was good enough for a second-place finish. He consistently hit for average, batting over .300 nine times and retiring with a lifetime average of .308. Ashburn was also a great fielder, as demonstrated by the fact that he routinely led the league in fielding percentage. Also, he had a good eye at the plate leading the league in walks four times, and he was an excellent base runner.

Ashburn was named to the National League All-Star Team five times (1948, 1951, 1953, 1958, and 1962). He finished his career with more than 2,500 hits. He had a reputation for being a spray hitter, meaning he could hit the ball to all parts of the diamond. This ability made it extremely difficult for opposing teams to defend him effectively when he had the bat in his hands.

Ashburn was nicknamed "Putt-Putt" by Ted Williams because he ran the bases so fast that you would think he had twin motors in his pants. Later he became known as "Whitey" due to his light blond hair. After he retired Harry Kalas (see *Keystone Tombstones Volume One*, Chapter 12), his broadcasting partner referred to Ashburn as "His Whiteness."

One of the great Richie Ashburn stories took place during a game played in 1957. Ashburn was at the plate when he fouled off a pitch into the stands. The ball hit Alice Roth, the wife of the *Philadelphia Bulletin* sports editor, square in the face. The impact not only stunned Mrs. Roth, but it also broke her nose. Play on the field was halted while medical personnel rushed to Mrs. Roth to help. After a quick examination, it was decided that she should be removed from the stadium using a stretcher. As Mrs. Roth was being carried out, play resumed, and Ashburn fouled off another pitch that struck the poor woman yet again. After the incident, Ashburn and Roth became friends and remained so for many years.

After the 1959 season, the Phillies traded Ashburn to the Chicago Cubs. He remained a Cub for two years before being selected by the New York Mets in the expansion draft of 1962. The original Mets who were described by their manager Casey Stengel as "amazing" may have been the worst team in the history of the major leagues. They finished the season with a record of 40–120, a dubious mark that no other team has been able to equal. While Ashburn had a good season and was named Most Valuable Met after hitting .305, the mountain of losses was too much for him to take. He retired at the end of the season and later re-marked, "I just didn't think I could go through another year like that."

Upon his retirement, Ashburn soon became a radio and television commentator for the Phillies. He also wrote sports columns for the *Philadelphia Bulletin* and later for the *Daily News*. Eventually, he was paired up with Harry Kalas to form the Phillies broadcasting team. The two became best friends as well as Philadelphia sports icons. Ashburn and Kalas called Phillies games for 27 years. Ashburn was known for his sense of humor as a broadcaster. He once told a story about a habit he had of keeping a bat that he was hitting well with in bed with him, so he was sure to have it for the next game. He ended the story by saying, "I slept with a lot of old bats in my day." He also liked to talk about how he felt about pitchers. "After fifteen years of facing them, you don't really get over them. They're devious. They're the only players in the game allowed to cheat. They throw illegal pitches, and they sneak foreign substances on the ball. They can inflict pain whenever they wish and, they're the only ones on the diamond who have high ground."

Years after he retired, Ashburn openly complained about being snubbed by the Baseball Writers Association in their voting to elect new members to the Baseball Hall of Fame. The three famous New York centerfielders, Willie, Mickey, and the Duke, were all quickly enshrined in the hall. Ashburn was thought to be left out because he was a singles hitter, unlike the sluggers from New York. That didn't stop Ashburn supporters from placing bumper stickers on their cars that read "Richie Ashburn: Why the Hall Not?" The efforts of Ashburn and his fans paid off as he was finally elected to the Hall of Fame in 1995.

On September 9, 1997, Ashburn finished broadcasting a Phillies-Mets game in New York City. He died of a heart attack later that night in his hotel room. There was a public viewing held in Fairmont Park that drew thousands of his admirers. The baseball fields in the park are named for him, as is the centerfield entertainment area at Citizens Bank Park; that area is known as Ashburn's Alley. His uniform number (1) was retired by the Phillies in 1979.

Richie Ashburn is buried in a modest grave in the Gladwyne Methodist Church Cemetery in Montgomery County. In 2005 a book titled *Richie Ashburn Remembered* was published. Harry Kalas penned the book's foreword.

If You Go:

Richie Ashburn's grave is in the Philadelphia area. Therefore, there are many other sites you may wish to visit that we covered in *Keystone Tombstones Volume One* as well as in this volume. After visiting Ashburn, you might want to take in the beautiful gravesite of his partner, Harry Kalas.

We were both hungry and thirsty after our visit to Ashburn's grave, so we stopped at the Stella Blue and the Star Bar in West Conshohocken. It proved to be a good choice. The bartender was friendly, and the food and drinks hit the spot. The bar has a sleek contemporary décor and an interesting and varied menu and drinks list. It looks like it would be a great spot in the evening, but we were there in the afternoon and had more to do. Hopefully, we can make it back there for a happy hour on one of our trips.

This tombstone marks the final resting place of baseball great Richie Ashburn who claimed that he slept with a lot of old bats during his baseball career.

2.

DE BONNEVILLE "BERT" BELL
"Modern Football's Founding Father"

County: Montgomery • Town: West Conshohocken
Buried at Calvary Cemetery
235 East Matsonford Road

In 1958, Bert Bell had one of his regular doctor appointments. His physician looked at him from behind his desk and advised Bell to avoid going to any more football games. Bell told his doctor that he'd much rather die at a football game than at home in bed. Although the Philadelphia Eagles held complimentary box seats for Bell and any guests he might have, he preferred buying his tickets and sitting with the other fans. On October 11, 1959, he was doing just that, sitting in the end zone watching the Eagles play the visiting Pittsburgh Steelers. In the fourth quarter, he suffered a heart attack and died later that day. He was sixty-four at the time.

Bert Bell was born in Philadelphia on February 25, 1895. Bert's father, John C. Bell, was a successful attorney who would eventually serve as Philadelphia's District Attorney and later as Attorney General of Pennsylvania. Bert's mother could trace her ancestors in America to before the American Revolution. His parents could only be described as very wealthy. He had one older brother, John C. Bell Jr., who would make quite a name for himself as well.

Bell's father went to the University of Pennsylvania, where he played the position of end on the football team. When Bert was six years old, his father took him to his first football game at Penn, and the young boy fell in love with the game. As he grew older, he attended various schools until he was ready for high school when he enrolled in the Haverford

Bert Bell circa 1925.

School. He was a tremendous sports star at Haverford, and in his senior year, he captained the school's football, basketball, and baseball teams. While baseball was his best sport, football was still his favorite. It was at this time that Bert's father was named a trustee for life at Penn. While serving in this position, he helped form the NCAA. When asked about

Bert's college plans, his father was clear, and to the point, he said, "Bert will go to Penn, or he will go to hell."

It should come with little surprise that Bert Bell entered Penn in the fall of 1914. That year he became the starting quarterback for the freshman team. The following year, Coach George Brooke selected Bell to be the starting varsity quarterback, which was quite an accomplishment for a sophomore. He also played as a defender, punter, and punt returner. By mid-season, Coach Brooke decided to use a two-quarterback system that did not have the desired results. The coach then resigned his position before the eighth game of the year, and Penn ended the season with a 3-5-2 record.

Later in life, Bell would tell a story about a train ride he took around this time. Following a Penn game, Bell boarded a train and found a seat next to an older man. The man looked at Bell and asked if he'd seen the game today. Bell nodded, yes. That set his fellow passenger off, "Isn't Bell the lousiest thing you ever saw?" He began to answer, but the passenger was far from finished. He described Bell as a safety that couldn't catch a punt and a punter who kicked the ball backward over his head. He went on to say that the only reason Bell was on the team was because of his dad's money and influence. The man was still railing on young Bell's performance when the train pulled into the passenger's station. The man got up to leave, held out his hand, and provided Bell with his name. The man then asked for Bert's name. Taking the man's hand and shaking it, the young quarterback responded, "Bert Bell."

Bell's mother died in September 1916 while he was on his way to say his final goodbyes to her. This didn't cause him to miss the start of the Penn football season playing for new coach Bob Folwell. Once again, his performance was inconsistent, and Folwell turned to a two-quarterback system. The team's record improved to 7-2-1, and after both Harvard and Yale turned down an invitation to the 1917 Rose Bowl, Penn was offered the chance and accepted. Penn's opponent in the game was the Oregon Ducks. While Penn piled up slightly more yardage than Oregon and Bell had the largest gain from scrimmage measuring 20 yards, he threw a key interception in the fourth quarter that led to a 14–0 Oregon win.

In 1917 Bell had his best year leading Penn to a 9–2 record. In December of that year, after "the war to end all wars" had drawn in the United States, he was inducted into the United States Army. After a few months of training, he was sent to France. Bell performed well in the war, and he volunteered for more than one dangerous mission. He ended up being promoted to sergeant, and at the war's end, he returned to the United States in March of 1919. That year he was named captain of the Penn football team, but his inconsistent play continued to plague him, and his team finished with a 6-2-1 record. His college career was over, and he was considered to have been an average player. His performance in the classroom was less than average; he failed to apply himself, and as a result, he left Penn without a degree.

Bell decided to stay in football and became an assistant coach at Penn. By all reports, he was highly regarded as an assistant and received several head coaching offers. He turned these down, believing that a head coach's job took up too much time. Before the 1929 season, Bell resigned from his position at Penn, and his father got him a job managing the Ritz Carleton Hotel. He also became a stockbroker during this period and managed to lose about $50,000 when the market crashed. His father came to his aid and took care of his losses.

Late in 1929, he accepted a position as an assistant coach at Temple University in Philadelphia. He served as the backfield coach from 1930 through 1932. In 1933 Temple hired Pop Warner as the head football coach, and he let Bell go. Bell enjoyed his life as an assistant using his free time to socialize and gamble. He loved the Saratoga Racecourse and visited there every year. While at Saratoga, he enjoyed hanging out with the Vanderbilts, Tim Mara, the Whitneys, and Art Rooney.

George Preston Marshall urged Bell to purchase a National Football League (NFL) franchise in 1932. In Bell's view, the college game was far more popular, so he dismissed the idea. By 1933, for some reason, he had changed his mind and decided he would buy a team. The NFL was interested in having a team in Pennsylvania, but the league informed Bell that the problem was the Pennsylvania blue laws that prohibited games being played on Sunday. Bell convinced Art Rooney to apply for an NFL franchise while he went to work on Pennsylvania's Governor Gifford Pinchot (for more information on Pinchot, see *Keystone Tombstones Volume One*, Chapter 22). Convincing Pinchot to change the laws would be no easy task. The Governor favored prohibition and was disappointed when the ban against liquor sales was repealed. Pinchot viewed the blue laws yet another roadblock making it more difficult for the public to purchase liquor. Bell's efforts resulted in the governor's consent to a bill that would allow local communities to determine the extent of the blue laws in their municipalities through referendums. The Pennsylvania General Assembly passed the bill in April of 1933, and the governor signed it into law.

Bell now needed monetary backing to buy a team. He went to his father, who refused because he disapproved of his son's choice to make football a career. Bell moved on without his father, borrowing the money from Frances Upton, a Broadway actress and devout Roman Catholic whom he would eventually secretly marry. The couple would have three children together, two boys and a girl. Bell would also convert to Catholicism in the last year of his life. The conversion was a result of the consistent urging of his wife as well as his long friendship with another Catholic by the name of Art Rooney. Bell partnered with Lud Wray, a fellow college assistant coach and others to purchase the Frankford Yellow Jackets. Bell and his partners renamed the team the Philadelphia Eagles and paid the NFL a $2,500 entrance fee.

The voters in Philadelphia passed a referendum easing the blue laws. Wray became the Eagles head coach, and Bell became the club's president. As president, he negotiated a deal with the Baker Bowl, an 18,500-seat stadium, to serve as the Eagles' home field. In their initial season in the league, the Eagles finished 3-5-1. In 1934 they improved slightly to 4–7, but 1935 saw their record drop to 2–9. Because the Eagles could not compete with the rest of the league, ticket sales fell, and between 1933 and 1935, the franchise had lost approximately $85,000. Bell grew frustrated because the best players were signing with the teams that had the most money. In his view, the only way the league could achieve parity would be for all the teams to have an equal shot at signing new players.

On May 18, 1935, a league meeting was held where Bell proposed that the league institute a draft system to level the competitive playing field and ensure that all teams would remain financially viable. The league adopted Bell's proposal without objection. The following year the first NFL draft was held. Of course, it continues to this day. One must wonder what Bell would think of his creation and the fan magnet it has become. ESPN covers the draft every year, and it gets excellent television ratings.

In 1936 the Eagles were sold through a public auction, and Bell became sole owner. Because of the team's financial situation, Bell let Wray go, and he assumed coaching duties himself. Also, he moved the Eagles home field to Municipal Stadium, which could house over 100,000 fans. In the 1936 season that Bell coached, the Eagles finished 1–11, which represented their poorest showing ever. The following year was not much better as the team came in with a record of 2-8-1. In 1938, Bell had his best year, finishing 5–6, and the franchise made a $7,000 profit. However, the Eagles could not maintain this momentum, and in 1939 they finished 1-9-1. They followed that with a 1–10 record.

In November of 1940, Bell got in touch with Pittsburgh Steeler owner Art Rooney and informed him that Alexis Thompson had approached him about buying the Eagles. Rooney, who had consistently lost money with the Steeler franchise, now saw a way out. He convinced the Steelers' board of directors to offer Bell a twenty percent commission for negotiating the sale of the Steelers to Thompson. Bell's efforts proved successful, and Rooney sold his team for about $165,000. As soon as the sale went through, Rooney purchased fifty percent of the Eagles. It was decided that Rooney would be the general manager, and Bell would continue as the coach.

Next came a series of events that Pennsylvania sports historians refer to as the "Pennsylvania Polka." In April of 1941, it was announced that the Eagles would be moving to Pittsburgh and play under the name of the Steelers, and at the same time, Thompson would move his team to Philadelphia, and they would be called the Eagles. The Steelers lost their first two games of the 1941 season, and Rooney convinced Bell to resign as coach. His career record was 10-46-2, and for coaches with at least five years at the helm, nobody had done worse.

As World War II drew more and more men into the Armed Forces, there were fewer players available to play football. Some owners wanted to shut down the league until the war ended, but Bell was against that proposal, noting that Major League Baseball was continuing to operate. In 1943 it got so bad that the Steelers and the Eagles were forced to combine roosters and create a team known as the Steagles. Bell continued to suffer financially during his partnership with Rooney, and Rooney eventually bought him out and took complete control of the Steelers.

The fact that he was no longer an owner put Bell in a position to get the job where his influence on the NFL would be felt for years to come. In 1941 Elmer Layden (one of the legendary Four Horsemen of Notre Dame) was named Commissioner of the NFL. Many NFL owners felt they had been left out of the decision to hire Layden. More than a few of the owners believed that Arch Ward, the sports editor of the *Chicago Tribune*, was the man who got Layden the job. NFL owners were naturally upset when in September of 1944, Ward organized a group of investors to create a new league, the All-American Football Conference (AAFC), to compete against the NFL. Also, Ward had drawn the interest of several potential investors for the new league that included John Keeshin, a trucking executive from Chicago, oilmen James Breuil and Ray Ryan, former heavyweight boxing champion Gene Tunney and Lou Gehrig's widow, Eleanor. A league was indeed formed, and Jim Crowley, yet another of the Four Horseman (see *Keystone Tombstones Volume One*, Chapter 6), was named commissioner.

Some NFL owners felt that Layden had a conflict of interest with dealing properly relative to the AAFC since, in their view, Ward had been his benefactor. Besides, some of the owners didn't believe that Layden took the new league seriously as a threat, nor did he appear concerned with the rise in players' salaries due to the competition between the leagues. As a result, Layden was fired on January 11, 1946, and Bell was chosen to replace him.

It didn't take long before Bell faced his first crisis. Dan Reeves, the owner of the Cleveland Browns, asked for permission to move his team to Los Angeles. The other owners denied his request. Reeves threatened to disband his team, and Bell was forced to step in. The new commissioner negotiated a settlement that resulted in the creation of the Los Angeles Rams.

Gambling had been a concern of the NFL ever since the league was established. Early in Bell's tenure, he was forced to face the issue. The day before the 1946 Championship game, two New York Giant players, Frank Filchock and Merle Hapes, were accused of having been offered bribes by a man named Alvin Paris in exchange for fixing the game. The Mayor of New York at the time was William O'Dwyer, and he informed the owner of the Giants and Bell of the evidence that had been gathered against the two players. The players were brought to the mayor's residence, where O'Dwyer interviewed them separately. Hapes admitted he had been offered money to fix the game, and Filchock denied the charge. The authorities quickly arrested Paris, who confessed to the charges against him. Bell suspended Hapes, but he allowed Filchock to play in the championship. When Paris went to jail and Filchock was put under oath at Paris's trial, Filchock admitted he had been offered a bribe.

After this incident, Commissioner Bell moved against gamblers. He worked with state legislatures throughout the country, urging them to pass legislation to make it illegal to fix games. His brother John, by this time, was the Lieutenant Governor of Pennsylvania (he would later serve as a Justice and then become the Chief Justice of the Pennsylvania Supreme Court), and he promised to lobby the Pennsylvania General Assembly to enact strict gambling laws. Bell himself wrote an antigambling resolution that he was successful in having added to the league constitution. This resolution gave the league commissioner the authority to permanently ban players for betting on a game or failing to inform league officials if they knew of any game being possibly fixed. Bell immediately used this power to ban Hapes and Filchock from the league. In July of 1947, Bell mandated that each team had to publish an injury report 48 hours before each game. The report was to include information on what players would not or may not play. The purpose of this move was to deny gamblers inside information. To this day, the NFL still requires teams to publish injury reports before every game.

The next problem that Commissioner Bell found on his plate was the threat of a new league: the AAFC. Ever since the establishment of the league was announced, it had hurt the pocketbooks of NFL franchise owners. Both leagues were in a battle for the best talent, and as a result, NFL payrolls had increased by 250 percent. Also, the AAFC outdrew the NFL in terms of attendance in both 1947 and 1948. However, nobody was making money; for three years in a row, neither league made a profit. Bell convinced most of the owners to allow him to open negotiations with the AAFC. On December 9, 1949, Bell emerged victoriously; he reached a settlement with the AAFC that removed the competition and, at the same time, merged three former AAFC teams into the NFL. Under the agreement, Bell would remain as commissioner, and the Cleveland Browns, the San Francisco 49ers, and the Baltimore Colts would join the NFL. The owners were so pleased with the settlement that they extended Bell's contract by five years.

As the number of television sets in American homes began to increase in the late 1940s and then skyrocket in the 1950s, the rights to televise the games and the NFL's blackout policy became a major issue. Bell felt, and he informed the owners of his opinion, that televising home games locally hurt the sale of tickets to the game. As a result, the NFL blacked-out home games to local television stations, except for the Los Angeles Rams, for the entire season in 1950. In response, the United States Justice Department opened an investigation of the league to determine if there had been a violation of the Sherman Antitrust Act. By the end of the season, the Rams, who broadcast all their home games, saw their home attendance plummet by fifty percent. Before the start of the 1951 season, Bell put the blackout rule back into effect. It was the commissioner's view that if you gave the game to fans for free on TV, you couldn't expect them to come to the stadium. This position led to the Justice Department filing suit against the NFL. The case was scheduled for trial in January 1952.

The Rams decided to blackout their home games for the 1951 season, and attendance increased back to its 1949 levels. After the 1951 season, Bell obtained the authority to set the television policy for every NFL team. He worked out a deal with the DuMont Television Network, which awarded that network the right to do a national broadcast of one NFL game a week. Bell took the revenue from the deal and divided it equally among all the NFL teams. This worked out to about $50,000 per team. That November, a judge ruled in the Justice Department case. The ruling found that Bell could not institute a policy that blacked out all NFL games. However, the judge also found that each NFL team was free to determine its policy relative to blackouts. Bell was more than pleased with the decision.

Setting up the NFL schedule had been an issue with the owners since the day the league was established. In the thirties, the league president set up the schedule. The president at the time held the philosophy that any schedule should favor the large city teams. Eventually, the owners took back the responsibility of setting the schedule, and this led to numerous disagreements as each owner fought for a schedule that would most benefit their team. Finally, in 1948 the owners gave Bell the authority to schedule. Bell decided that early in the season, weak teams would play weak teams, and the strong teams would also play each other. Bell felt that attendance would be helped if the differences in team standings could be minimized if possible.

Bell and the NFL found themselves back in the courts in the 1950s. This case involved a former player for the Detroit Lions named Bill Radovich. Radovich was one of the NFL players who left the league to play in the AAFC. The NFL passed a rule that banned any of these players from working for the NFL for five years. After playing in the AAFC for two years, Radovich was offered a job with the San Francisco Clippers, a Pacific Coast League team that was affiliated with the NFL. The NFL warned the Clippers that there would be sanctions if they hired Radovich, and as a result, the Clippers withdrew their job offer. Radovich responded by filing suit against the NFL seeking damages. The case gradually worked its way through the judicial system. Bell's brother, John, who by now was the Chief Justice of the Pennsylvania Supreme Court, told his brother that the NFL case was a losing one. Bell's brother's judgment proved correct, and in 1957 the United States Supreme Court ruled in favor of Radovich. The loss of the individual case was not what Bell found alarming about the decision. What concerned him was that the Supreme Court had ruled that the NFL was subject to antitrust laws.

Congress immediately set hearings to study the effect of the ruling. Bell argued through the media that the NFL was a sport and not a business and, therefore, not subject to antitrust laws. Representatives of the NFL Players Association (NFLPA, the players union) appeared before Congress and took the position that both the NFL draft and the reserve clause were anti-labor and needed to be eliminated. Seeing that Congress was going to become involved in the running of the NFL, Bell formally recognized the Players Association, and the crisis passed.

While all this was going on, professional football continued to gain a larger share of the American audience. The 1958 NFL championship was much anticipated though no one knew at the time that it would mark a surge in the NFL's popularity that would take the league to the top of the sports market in the United States. The championship was scheduled to be played in historic Yankee Stadium on December 28, 1958. Ironically, the game that provided the foundation for football to pass baseball as America's favorite sport was played in the House that Ruth Built.

The two teams who would face each other were the Baltimore Colts and the New York Giants. To give you an idea of how star-studded this game was, seventeen individuals (including coaches) involved in the contest are current members of the Pro Football Hall of Fame. The Giants fielded Sam Huff and Frank Gifford and had a defensive coordinator by the name of Tom Landry and an offensive coordinator named Vince Lombardi. Baltimore was led by a quarterback named Johnny Unitas, defensive lineman Gino Marchetti, and a running back/wide receiver named Lenny Moore. Bell somehow sensed the importance of the contest, and he lifted the NFL blackout rules; the game would be televised nationally.

The game lived up to its billing. The Giants were ahead 17–14 late in the fourth quarter when they punted the ball to the Baltimore 14-yard line. Unitas then led one of the most famous drives in NFL history. He threw two incomplete passes before connecting with Moore for an 11-yard gain. After missing with another pass, he connected with Raymond Berry three straight times, putting the ball on the Giant 13-yard line with just seven seconds left in the game. The Colts kicked a 20-yard field goal, and the game was sent into sudden-death overtime. The Giants won the toss and took the ball first in the overtime, but they were unable to get a first down, so they punted. Unitas once again led the Colts down the field on a 13-play 80-yard drive that ended when Alan Ameche scored on a third-down run from the one-yard line to give the Colts the championship by a score of 23–17. This would be the last NFL championship Bell would ever witness, and he viewed it as the culmination of a life's work. By the conclusion of the game, the commissioner was in tears.

As mentioned previously, Bell died the following year. His funeral was held in Saint Margaret Roman Catholic Church on October 14, 1959. Dignitaries, friends, and admirers attended the funeral mass. The owners of the NFL teams and the President of the Green Bay Packers served as honorary pallbearers. Bell was laid to rest at Calvary Cemetery in West Conshohocken, Pennsylvania.

After Bell's death, the great sportswriter, Red Smith, noted, "He was watching the Eagles, the team he had created with his own sweat and tears and money, playing his other team, the Steelers, which he operated with Art Rooney during the war. They were playing on Franklin Field,

Here lies the man who may be responsible for making professional football America's national pastime.

where forty years earlier, a little Penn quarterback had played the game that was to become his life. It was almost as though he could choose the time and place."

If You Go:

Calvary Cemetery is a Mecca for sports fans. Alan Dante "The Horse" Ameche was laid to rest there in 1988. Ameche won the 1954 Heisman Trophy as a running back at Wisconsin. He was drafted in the first round by the Baltimore Colts, and on his first NFL play, he went seventy-nine yards for a touchdown. He was the 1955 NFL Rookie of the Year. Ameche is best remembered for scoring the winning touchdown in overtime to give the Colts the championship in the 1958 final played in Yankee Stadium. Yes, Ameche scored the touchdown that left Bert Bell in tears. How ironic is it that they are buried in the same cemetery?

You can also find Francis James Bagnell at Calvary. He was an All-American football player at the University of Pennsylvania. He won the Maxwell Trophy and finished second in the voting for the Heisman. He is a member of the College Football Hall of Fame.

Henry Charles ("Shag") Crawford was buried at Calvary in 2007. Crawford was a catcher in the minor leagues, and when his playing career ended, he became an umpire. He would umpire over 3,000 games between 1956 and 1975. Well respected in the game, he worked three World Series and two National League Championship Series.

Finally, the much-respected NFL referee Stanley Javie can also be found at Calvary. Javie worked for the NFL from 1951 to 1980, and he was selected to referee four Super Bowls. Calvary is a large cemetery, so the authors suggest a visit to the cemetery office where you can get directions to the sites.

If you visit Calvary, you are not far from the final resting place of baseball great Richie Ashburn (see Chapter 1 in this volume). Also, you are very close to Philadelphia, where you can visit the graves of the people covered in this volume, as well as those that can be found in *Keystone Tombstones Volume One*.

3.

SMEDLEY BUTLER

"The Fighting Quaker"

County: Chester • Town: West Chester
Buried at Oaklands Cemetery
1042 Pottstown Pike

Smedley Darlington Butler, nicknamed "the fighting Quaker," was a major general in the United States Marine Corps and, at the time of his death, the most decorated Marine in United States history. Butler was a double recipient of the Congressional Medal of Honor, one of only twenty people to ever be so decorated. He is one of three to be awarded the Marine Corps Brevet Medal and the Medal of Honor and the only man to be awarded the Brevet Medal and two Medals of Honor, all for separate actions. During his 34-year career as a Marine, he participated in military actions in the Philippines, China, Central America, the Caribbean, and France in World War I. By the end of his career he had received sixteen medals, five of which were for heroism. Yet his military career is only part of what makes his story so very interesting.

Butler was born in West Chester, Pennsylvania, and was the Quaker son of Thomas Stalker Butler, who was a lawyer, judge, and for 31 years a congressman. During the Spanish American War, Butler left high school 38 days before his 17th birthday to enlist in the Marine Corps. Although he did not finish all the coursework, he was awarded his high school diploma on June 6, 1898.

In the anti-Spanish war fever of 1898, he lied about his age and received a direct commission as a Marine second lieutenant. He fought in the Philippine-American war later that year. In 1900, he received a brevet promotion to captain and the Marine Corps Brevet Medal for his action

Smedley Butler (left) in Shanghai.

during the Boxer Rebellion in which he was shot in the thigh and chest. In 1903 he fought to protect the United States Consulate in Honduras from rebels. Between the Honduras campaign and his next assignment, he returned to Philadelphia, and on June 30, 1905, he married Ethel Conway Peters. The couple would have three children: a daughter Ethel and two sons Smedley and Thomas.

Butler served in Nicaragua from 1909 to 1912, and then in 1914, he earned his first Medal of Honor for the capture of Veracruz, Mexico, during the Mexican Revolution. The citation says he exhibited courage and skill in leading his men.

The following year he was ordered to Haiti when Haitian rebels, known as "Cacos," killed the Haitian dictator Vilbrun Sam. The Marines captured the rebel stronghold, Fort Riviere, after engaging in hand-to-hand combat. Butler's performance impressed the Assistant Secretary of the Navy, Franklin D. Roosevelt, who recommended him for his second Medal of Honor, which was presented to him in 1917. That made him and Dan Daly the only Marines to receive the Congressional Medal of Honor twice for separate actions.

During World War I, he was promoted to the rank of brigadier general and placed in command of Camp Pontanezen at Brest, France, a debark station depot. His performance there earned him the Distinguished Service Medal of both the United States Army and Navy and the French Order of the Black Star.

After World War I, he became the Commanding General of the Marine Barracks at Quantico, Virginia. During a training exercise in 1921, he was told by a local farmer that Stonewall Jackson's arm was buried nearby. Not believing it, he had a squad of Marines dig up the spot and did indeed find Stonewall's arm in a wooden box. He replaced the wooden box with a metal box and reburied the arm. He left a plaque on the granite monument marking the place. The plaque is no longer on the market but can be viewed at the Chancellorsville Battlefield Visitor's Center.

In 1924 Butler was asked by the Major of Philadelphia, W. Freeland Kendrick, to become the city's Director of Public Safety. Philadelphia's municipal government was notoriously corrupt, and Butler initially refused. President Coolidge intervened and authorized the necessary leave from the Marines. His major problem was the enforcement of Prohibition, and his strong enforcement action earned him both enmity and respect. He left after two years and later stated that "cleaning up Philadelphia was worse than any battle I was ever in."

In 1927 Butler served a tour in China and returned as a major general in 1929. In 1931 he publicly recounted a story about Benito Mussolini in which Mussolini struck a child with his automobile and refused to stop. This story caused international outrage, and Butler was arrested and court-martialed. The source of the story turned out to be Cornelius Vanderbilt Jr., who years later substantially confirmed the story. Butler was ordered to apologize to Mussolini, but he refused. Secretary of State Stimson issued a formal apology to Mussolini. As a trial approached, the case was settled by Butler receiving a reprimand. He retired on October 1, 1931.

In 1932 he ran for the United States Senate as a proponent of Prohibition but was defeated in the Republican primary by James Davis. During his campaign, Butler spoke forcefully about the veteran's bonus for service during WW I. He spoke to the famous "Bonus Army" that marched on Washington and made camp nearby and encouraged them in their efforts. On July 28, 1932, army cavalry units led by General Douglas MacArthur dispersed the Bonus Army marchers and their wives and children by riding through Hooverville, as it came to be called, and using tear gas and burning their shelters and belongings. Butler then declared himself a "Hoover for ex-president Republican."

In 1934 Smedley Butler alleged the existence of a political conspiracy of Wall Street interests to overthrow President Roosevelt and that he had been asked to lead it. These allegations became known as the Business Plot. The allegations were never proven, but a Congressional investigation found that such an attempt was contemplated. (See *The Plot to Seize the Whitehouse* by Jules Archer)

Butler became known for his outspoken views against war profiteering. In 1935 he wrote his book *War is a Racket,* a condemnation of the profit motive behind warfare. His views are summarized in the following passage from a 1935 issue of the magazine *Common Sense*:

I spent 33 years and four months in active military service, and during that period, I spent most of my time as a high-class thug for Big Business, for Wall Street and the bankers. In short, I was a racketeer, a gangster for capitalism. I helped make Mexico and especially Tampico safe for American oil interests in 1914. I helped make Haiti and Cuba a decent place for the National City Bank boys to collect revenues in. I helped in the raping of half a dozen Central American republics for the benefit of Wall Street. I helped purify Nicaragua for the international banking house of Brown Brothers in 1902–1912. I brought light to the Dominican Republic for the American sugar interests in 1916. I helped make Honduras right for the American fruit companies in 1903. In China in 1927, I helped see to it that Standard Oil went on its way unmolested. Looking back on it, I might have given Al Capone a few hints. The best he could do was to operate his racket in three districts. I operated on three continents.

Butler fought hard to raise awareness of what the real motivating factors of war were. He tried to bring the economic implications of war to the forefront of the public conscience. "War is a racket. It always has been. It is possibly the oldest, easily the most profitable, surely the most vicious," he wrote, noting how proponents typically use God and freedom to explain the mission but never discuss the economic details:

It is conducted for the benefit of the very few at the expense of the masses. Like all members of the military profession, I never had a thought of my own until I left the service. My mental faculties remained in suspended animation while I obeyed the orders of higher-ups.

In June 1940, Butler checked himself into a hospital after becoming sick. His doctor described his illness as an incurable condition of the upper abdominal tract, presumably cancer. He died in the Naval Hospital in Philadelphia on June 21, 1940. He is buried in a modest grave in Oaklands Cemetery in West Chester, Pennsylvania.

The USS *Butler* was named in his honor in 1942. This destroyer participated in the European and Pacific theaters during WW II. It was later

Pictured above is the grave of two-time Medal of Honor Recipient Smedley Butler who showed courage on the battlefield and beyond.

converted to a high-speed minesweeper. The Marine base in Okinawa is named in his honor.

His books, *War Is A Racket* and *The Letters of a Leatherneck*, are still available as are many books about him. There is also a Smedley Butler Society at www.warisaracket.org.

In Soldiers' Grove, behind the Pennsylvania State Capitol Building in Harrisburg, Smedley Butler is memorialized with a headstone in the ground. All of Pennsylvania's Congressional Medal of Honor recipients are honored in this way.

If You Go:

There are several other interesting people buried in Oaklands Cemetery. Dewitt Clinton Lewis was a lieutenant colonel for the Union Army who received the Congressional Medal of Honor recipient for rescuing a private.

William Hollingsworth Whyte Jr., a graduate of Princeton, was the author of the 1956 bestseller *The Organization Man* and a pioneer in urban planning specifically related to public life and pedestrian behavior.

Joseph Emley Borden was the winning pitcher of the first Major League Baseball game ever played. He pitched for the Boston Red Caps, who beat the Philadelphia Athletics 6–5 on April 22, 1876.

Harry Dunn was an artist best known for creating the peacock logo for the NBC television network.

Samuel Barber was a two-time Pulitzer Prize-winning composer whose works included symphonies, operas, chamber music, and songs. His will stipulated that the burial plot neighboring his should be reserved for his long-time friend and partner, Glan Carlo Menotti, or, at the very least, have a stone inscribed "To the Memory of Two Friends." Menotti is buried in Scotland.

4.

MICHAEL CHESLOCK

"The Lattimer Massacre"

County: Luzerne • Town: Hazleton
Buried at Hazleton Cemetery
120 North Vine Street

On September 17, 1897, the *Hazleton Daily Standard* published the following verse:

> If the courts of justice shield you
> And your freedom you should gain,
> Remember that your brows are marked
> With the burning brand of Cain.
>
> Oh, noble, noble, deputies
> We always will remember
> Your bloody work at Lattimer
> On the 10th day of November.

The verse was a testament to yet another act of violence involving labor and management in the Coal Region of Pennsylvania. This incident became known as the Lattimer Massacre.

The Coal Region is in northeastern Pennsylvania. It is largely made up of six counties: Lackawanna, Luzerne, Columbia, Carbon, Schuylkill, and Northumberland. Coal was discovered in the area in 1762. This discovery would have a profound influence on those who chose to settle in the Coal Region in the 1800s. The coal industry went through a tremendous growth spurt after the Civil War. This growth provided tremendous wealth for the few who had the capital to obtain mining rights

Miners marching to their slaughter outside of Lattimer, Pennsylvania, September 10, 1897.

and the land beneath where the vast deposits of coal could be found. For a minority of people who worked for the mining companies, it provided a good job and a decent income. These people were mine bosses, superintendents, and supervisors. Most of the employees were the actual miners who were faced with extremely dangerous work, harsh conditions, and low pay coupled with the fact that they were forced to live in company supplied housing and purchase their goods at company-owned stores. Often a miner's wages failed to cover his and his family's expenses, and he went into debt to the company. These conditions led to conflict, sometimes violent, between labor and management (see *Keystone Tombstones Volume One*, Chapter 13 on the Molly Maguires).

The jobs in the mines were generally filled by the latest groups of immigrants to enter the region. This meant that in the 1890s, most of the miners were of Italian or Slavic descent. At this time, the company-owned town of Lattimer housed an Italian population. Slavic miners and their families largely occupied similar company-owned towns in the area. In either case, they were renting their homes from mine owner

30

Ariovistus Pardee, who was one of the wealthiest men in America at the time.

As newcomers, these miners were often assigned the most difficult and dangerous jobs available. Also, they were often subjected to prejudice. For example, the Slavic miners were often called "hunkies." They were also angry about the "alien tax" that had been passed by the Pennsylvania General Assembly. This tax required a three-cent levy per day on all immigrant employees. When one considers that the immigrants' earnings were already set lower than their more established counterparts doing the same work, it becomes easy to see the anger that resulted from these conditions. Thus, the stage had been set for the latest clash between labor and management in Pennsylvania's Coal Region.

Several incidents occurred in the late summer of 1897 that led to the trouble that would eventually take place in Lattimer. In August, Gomer James, who worked for the mine owners in a management position, decided to make a central stable for all the mules who worked in the mines to save money. Mine owners at this time valued a trained mule more than a miner since it cost about $200 to buy and train the animal. One of the savings was that a single crew could now be given the job of feeding and watering the mules. Another consequence of the decision was that the mules were no longer kept at the mines where they worked, and the mule drivers had to travel to the central stable to pick them up. In many cases, this added two hours to the workers' day as they had to wake an hour early to get to the stable to pick up the mule and then spend an hour after work returning the animal. The workers were angry because they received no compensation for this extra time.

On August 13, 1897, most of the mule drivers who worked at the Honeybrook mine went on strike. Also, they formed a human fence and refused to allow anyone to enter the mine to get to work. When word of this reached Jones, he grabbed a crowbar, rushed to the scene, and attacked the nearest striker, hitting him across the shoulders. The other strikers rushed to intervene and soon had Jones on the ground where they began to beat him. The local supervisor, Oliver Welsh, then intervened, stopping the beating and promptly firing all the strikers. In breaking up the fight, Welsh suffered a blow to the head from a stone; it took eight stitches to close the wound.

News of what happened at Honeybrook quickly spread across the coalfields. The result was that more miners joined the strike. Within three days, more than 800 miners had joined the effort to better their treatment. They demanded a wage hike, the right to shop at stores other than those owned by the company, the freedom to choose their doctor, and an end to the alien tax. The strikers appointed a team of leaders to negotiate with management on their behalf.

The strike ended temporarily when the strikers' leaders negotiated a ten-cent pay increase. While the miners were happy with the increase, they remained disturbed that their other issues had not been addressed, and as a result, on August 25, 1897, the strike was renewed with a march. Local newspapers reported that anywhere from 300 to 500 miners had taken to the streets to march in protest of their working conditions.

On September 4, 1879, the miners issued a list of demands. These demands included a fifteen cents per day raise for every employee, the right to seek out and pay for the doctor of their choice; they would be paid if they reported to work even if work wasn't possible because machinery was out of order; and they would not be compelled to shop in company stores or use the company butcher. The coal companies divided in their response to these demands. By September 6th, the men at Coleraine and Milnesville were back at work. The mine owners here agreed that the miners could shop where they wished though the company stores would remain open. That same day, Sheriff Martin of Luzerne County met with supervisors of the Cross Creek Coal Company, and it was decided that none of the strikers' demands would be met. The coal company agreed that it would furnish funds to pay for an armed force of deputies to aid the Coal and Iron Police. Sheriff Martin was dispatched to Hazleton with instructions to raise such a force. Martin had no trouble finding men, and within a day, he deputized approximately eighty volunteers who he armed with new Winchester rifles. Martin also issued a proclamation that he sent to the *Wilkes-Barre Times*. The proclamation put the striking miners on notice in that it warned against any unlawful assembly or any acts of violence.

On September 9th, a group of miners from Lattimer met with their counterparts from Harwood. The Harwood miners were already on strike, and the delegation from Lattimer expressed their desire to join in and close both of Pardee's mines in the area. The largely Slavic miners from Harwood agreed that Pardee would give no concessions unless he was faced with a show of unity from the miners. Therefore, it was

ANOTHER TRIAL CERTAIN

FOR SHERIFF MARTIN AND THE OTHER

LATTIMER MURDERERS.

Prosecutors Say the
County's Honor
Demands It.

Jury Feared Coal Barons
and Wouldn't Punish
"Best Families."

VERDICT IN ADVANCE.

So Also Was Judge's Charge.
Sheriff Tells What He'll
Do in Next Trouble.

WHAT *IS* CRIME IN PENNSYLVANIA ANYHOW?

It seems to t settled that in the mining regions deputy sheriffs have the right to kill unarmed strikers on sight. They may pursue them and shoot them down as they would mad dogs. And in the end the deputy sheriffs are glorified as martyrs—not hanged as murderers.

From the New York Evening Journal, *10 March 1898, p. 5.*

decided that the Harwood miners would march to Lattimer the next day, where the Lattimer miners would join them in the strike.

September 10, 1897, was a warm and sunny day. Approximately three hundred men appeared at Harwood to join in the march to Lattimer. A few of the men carried American flags to display during the march. Most of the marchers did not speak English, nor were they American citizens. Michael Cheslock, who did speak English and had applied for American citizenship, was selected to be one of the leaders of the march. The large group set off for Lattimer; they were unarmed and marched peacefully.

As soon as Sheriff Martin received word of the procession, he mobilized his forces. As the marchers neared Hazleton, they were met by Martin and his posse. Martin pulled his gun, pointed it at a marcher, and ordered the group to disperse. The miners, who felt they were doing nothing wrong, refused. Around this time, a fight broke out, and one deputy grabbed a flag from a marcher and tore it to bits. At this point, the chief of the Hazleton police intervened. The fighting stopped when the chief said the march could continue but could not go through Hazleton. The marchers agreed and proceeded on around the city.

Martin ordered his men to trolleys bound for Lattimer. Later some of the trolley passengers would report that tensions were high, and there was talk of a shooting. One deputy was overheard, saying, "I bet I drop six of them." A reporter notified the *Wilkes-Barre Times* that serious trouble was coming. Word of what was happening spread through the area. Mothers in Lattimer went to the local schoolhouse to remove their children, a wise move considering what was about to unfold. The Lattimer mine shut down. Martin and his men arrived and were joined by coal and iron police. Now in command of an armed force of about 150, Martin assembled his men at the forked entrance to the town of Lattimer.

It was 3:45 that afternoon when the marchers approached Lattimer led by a man carrying the American flag. The miners' ranks had by now swelled to over 400 men. Martin approached the marchers and told them they were participating in an unlawful assembly. He ordered them to disperse. Many of the marchers couldn't understand what the sheriff said, and just as many could not hear him. Michael Cheslock and other leaders of the march attempted to talk with Martin, but the sheriff was having none of that. He attempted to grab the American flag from the marcher in front. Failing there, he grabbed a marcher from the second row, and when other marchers came to his defense, a scuffle ensued. Martin pulled his pistol, but it misfired, and at this point, someone yelled, "fire." Eyewitnesses would claim it was the sheriff, but he would deny the charge. Whoever gave the order, the deputies fired. Michael Cheslock was shot between the eyes and killed immediately. The marchers, seeing what was happening, turned to run, but the deputies continued to fire. Some ran toward the schoolhouse, where the teachers inside soon saw shots piercing the walls and splintering the wood. The shooting went on for at least a minute and a half, and when it was over, 19 of the marchers lay dead and another thirty-six were wounded. Some of the deputies walked through the dead and wounded, kicking them. Some of the marchers begged for help, and one eyewitness heard a deputy respond to these pleas by saying, "We'll give you hell, not water, hunkies!" Sheriff Martin surveyed the area around him, and in a classic understatement, muttered, "I am not well."

Wagons were called in to move the dead and wounded to local hospitals and undertakers. Many of the dead were taken to Boyle's and Bonin's who, as undertakers, were assigned the responsibility of preparing the bodies for burial. Undertaker Boyle would later testify that the bodies left in his care had been shot in the back. (Note: Boyle's descendants run a funeral home in Hazleton to this day. The funeral director at present is named Thomas Boyle. He and the author went to high school together.)

The next few days were bedlam in the coal country—many of the deputies headed to the Jersey Shore to wait out the events. The Governor of Pennsylvania sent the state militia to Hazleton to preserve order since most expected there would be reprisals. To the surprise of many, the immigrants remained peaceful. Large funerals continued in the days to follow, some drawing crowds of as many as eight thousand people.

FIRING ON THE MINERS. AN ACCURATE VIEW OF THE FIELD WHERE THE TRAGEDY TOOK PLACE
Drawn by an Inquirer Staff Artist.

By a Philadelphia Inquirer *staff person, 12 September 1897, front page.*

The story of the massacre was covered in the press throughout the country. Generally, the sheriff and his deputies were found to be at fault. *The Philadelphia Inquirer* said that the massacre was,

a human slaughter in which men were mowed down like grain stalks before a scythe, by the deadly bullets which stormed for fully two minutes. An exact list of the dead and wounded is impossible to be obtained tonight, but the *Inquirer* counted twelve dead men in the field. Two others died at the hospital, and several others are expected to die at any moment.

The press was hounding sheriff Martin, so he finally told his side of the story. He said he received word of the march from one of his deputies who told him that the miners were heavily armed. In response, he gathered his deputies together and told them to remain calm no matter what happened. He said when the marchers arrived in Lattimer, he read them the proclamation but that they paid no attention to him and continued to march. Martin said he told the leader to stop, but that order was also ignored. He said he tried to arrest the leader, but when he did, he was surrounded by the strikers who began kicking him. He then told the reporters,

> I realized something needed to be done at once, or I would
> be killed. I called to the deputies to discharge their firearms
> into the air over the heads of the strikers, as it might probably
> frighten them. It was done at once, but it had no effect
> whatever on the infuriated foreigners, who used me so much
> the rougher and became fiercer and fiercer, more like wild beasts
> than human beings.

Martin went on to say that the miners were desperate and did not value human life. He claimed that his deputies were ordered to shoot only to protect their own lives and the property they were there to defend. He said that he felt bad about giving the order to fire but insisted that it was his duty considering the situation.

Soon after this interview, Martin changed his story. He said the marchers were not on company property; that they were on a public road. When asked if the marchers had done anything that was not peaceful, he said no. He denied giving the order to fire, saying that had been done by someone else. Soon after, Martin and his deputies were arrested and charged with murder.

On February 1, 1898, the trial of Martin and his deputies began in Wilkes-Barre. It took over a month to complete, and testimony was

This monument sits at the site of the massacre.

*The grave site of Michael Cheslock who was the first miner
killed during the Lattimer Massacre.*

received from about 200 witnesses. On March 9, 1898, the jury returned with a verdict of "not guilty." News of the verdict sparked outrage not only in the United States but throughout Eastern Europe as well. A Slovak cartoon shows a dead miner laying at the feet of justice. Justice is not depicted as being blind but is seen looking at a bag of money.

In many ways, the martyred miners of Lattimer inspired the working people of America to do something about their working conditions. After the massacre, more than 15,000 workers joined the United Mine Workers of America. In time that union became the most powerful representative of the anthracite workers. At the peak of its power, it represented 150,000 workers in the region.

In 1972 a monument was erected in Lattimer at the site of the massacre. An inscription on the monument reads,

> It was not a battle because they were not aggressive, nor were they defensive because they had no weapons of any kind and were simply shot down like so many worthless objects, each of the licensed life-takers trying to outdo the others in butchery.

Michael Cheslock is buried in Hazleton Cemetery. His grave is easy to find if you use the Diamond Avenue entrance. As you enter, Cheslock's grave is to your right just a few yards away from your entry point. Cheslock was 39 years old when he was killed.

Here lay four of fourteen victims of the massacre buried side by side.

If You Go:

Also buried in Hazleton Cemetery is Sergeant Robert H. Sinex, who fought with the Union during the Civil War. According to one of his death notices, he was a secret service agent who saw Lincoln's assassination and participated in the capture of John Wilkes Booth. If you wish to visit his grave, we suggest a stop at the cemetery office. Hazleton Cemetery is located on the same side of town as the Saint Stanislaus's Polish Catholic Cemetery, and a visit to this site is a must. Fourteen of the miners shot at Lattimer are buried here in a manner to get your attention. The fourteen are lined up side by side against the cemetery wall. Their tombstones are identical, and all contain the same information. At the top of the stone is the miner's name and inscribed underneath the name on each marker it reads, "Shot September 10, 1897."

This cemetery is located at 652 Carson Street in Hazleton, and the wall you are looking for is the one with the school building right across the street. If you visit Saint Stanislaus's, you are right next to the Most Precious Blood Cemetery. You may want to stop here to visit the grave of Jack "the Dandy" Parisi. Parisi was a member of the notorious group Murder Incorporated, which accepted and carried out murder contracts from mob bosses throughout the country. A government agent once said of Parisi, "if you hung him up by his thumbs for eight hours, he might tell you his name."

If you need refreshments, you have plenty of options in Hazleton. We had a pint and the best perogies we have ever tasted at a small pub called the Battered Mug located on the corner of South Pine and Beech

These fourteen tombstones lined up side by side mark the graves of miners shot to death during the massacre.

streets. If you are in Hazleton, you are close to many people that we covered in *Keystone Tombstones Volume One,* including Jim Thorpe, "Black Jack" Kehoe of the Molly Maguires, Congressman Dan Flood, and Mary Jo Kopechne. As it would be very difficult to visit all the sites in one day, we recommend spending the night at the Comfort Inn located in West Hazleton. The hotel is clean, reasonably priced, and has friendly staff. Besides, it houses a nice lounge called Timbers that offers live entertainment on the weekends.

5.

BILLY CONN
"The Pittsburgh Kid"

County: Allegheny • Town: Pittsburgh
Buried at Calvary Catholic Cemetery
718 Hazelwood Avenue

On May 18, 1941, Joe Louis, the undisputed heavyweight champion of the world, stepped into the ring at the Polo Grounds to defend his title for the 18th time. Louis had trained hard for this fight wanting to lose weight and gain speed. At the morning weigh-in, he tipped the scales at just under 200 pounds. Looking across the ring at his opponent, Louis saw a much smaller man. The challenger had weighed in at 169 pounds and was a decided underdog. He had given up his light heavyweight crown to earn the right to fight Louis. His name was Billy Conn, the Pittsburgh Kid, and he was about to capture the hearts of the American public.

Conn was born on October 8, 1917, in Pittsburgh, Pennsylvania. Pittsburgh of that day was far different from the city today. It was the steel city then, and with all the black smoke coming from the mills, the streetlights were kept on during the day. H. L. Mencken described it as "so dreadfully hideous, so intolerably bleak and forlorn that it reduced the whole aspiration of a man to a macabre and depressing joke."

Conn's father, Billy Sr., worked in those mills for forty years. He once told his son that one day he would have a job at the plant. The very idea was enough to scare Conn into pursuing another career. Years later, he talked about how people always said you had to be crazy to be a fighter. In Conn's words, "I was nuts, but it beats working in those mills."

Conn's parents sent him to parochial school at a place called Sacred Heart. He lasted until the 8th grade when one of the nuns suggested that

Billy Conn

another child could make far better use of the space he was taking up. By this time, Conn had already gotten a job in a gym where his primary duty was as a janitor. The job did provide him with the opportunity to spar and served as his introduction to boxing.

Conn never fought a single fight as an amateur. His manager, Johnny Ray, didn't believe in fighting unless there was a purse at stake. When he was 17, Conn fought professionally for the first time. He went four rounds but lost on a decision to a more experienced opponent. He was paid $1.50 for the bout. He lost a few more fights in 1935, but within a couple of years, he grew as both a fighter and a man. By 1937 he weighed 147 pounds and had developed a solid left jab and a hook that Joe Louis would describe as the fastest he had ever seen.

In 1936 Conn won a bout against a future welterweight champ by the name of Fritzie Zivic. Zivic was also from Pittsburgh, and the two fighters disliked each other; it was a local rivalry. During round one, Zivic used the laces of his gloves on Conn, who responded in round two with a shot to Zivic's groin. The fight went a full ten rounds with Conn emerging the winner by decision. Conn later called Zivic the dirtiest fighter he ever faced. Zivic was one of ten future boxing champions who would lose a fight to the Pittsburgh Kid. This win put Conn on the boxing map from which he would never disappear.

Conn continued to compete against very tough fighters; he never ducked anyone. Once, Pittsburgh Pirate announcer Bob Prince (see *Keystone Tombstones Volume One*, Chapter 23) said on air that Conn had ducked opponents. Conn saw Prince at the Pittsburgh Arena, slammed him into a wall, and said he'd beat the hell out of him if he kept up the negative and false reporting. Prince held his tongue, and the two became good friends.

On May 27, 1937, he faced a black boxer by the name of Oscar Rankin. He won his 23rd straight fight that night. It was years later that Joe Louis told Conn that his managers had refused to let him fight Rankin. Louis told Conn, "the people who managed you must not have liked you very much. Nobody would let me fight that sonuvabitch."

By the year 1939, Conn was reaching his prime. He fought Fred Apostoli, who would later become the middleweight champion of the world, twice early in the year with both bouts taking place at Madison Square Garden. Conn won both fights by decision. One of the spectators at the first bout was a beautiful young woman by the name of Mary Louise Smith. Conn first met Mary when she was fifteen, and he immediately informed her that one day he was going to marry her. Mary's father, Jimmy Smith, who played second base for the 1917 World Series champion New York Giants, didn't approve. He vowed he would never let Conn marry his daughter. A few years later, in 1941, Conn and Mary Louise Smith became man and wife, despite her father's wishes.

On July 13, 1939, Conn met Melio Bettina for the Light Heavyweight Championship of the world. After 15 hard-fought rounds, Conn emerged the winner. A rematch was set for September 25, 1939. It took another 15 rounds, but Conn successfully defended his title. The number one heavyweight contender at this time was Bob Pastor, who had only been defeated once, by Joe Louis, in over 50 fights. On September 6, 1940, Conn fought Pastor in New York City. It was yet another tough fight, but in the 13th round, Conn knocked Pastor to the canvas where he was counted out. Conn was now the number one contender for the heavyweight crown. Conn would remain the Light Heavyweight Champion until May of 1941 when he voluntarily relinquished the title to pursue the Heavyweight Championship of the World.

On the night of June 18, 1941, the Pittsburgh Pirates had a night game at home. The Pirates' management knew that everyone in Pittsburgh was going to stay home to listen to the broadcast of the Pittsburgh Kid taking on Joe Louis. To draw fans to the ballpark, the Pirates announced that once the fight began, the game would be halted, and the radio broadcast would be played through the stadium's public address system.

Conn entered the ring an enormous underdog. Not only was he much smaller than Louis, but he was facing a man many considered (and many still do) the greatest heavyweight fighter in history. Joe Louis was certainly confident of his place in boxing history, as he demonstrated when he appeared on a television show with Muhammad Ali shortly after Ali became champion. Ali asked Louis if he thought he could have won a fight between the two. Louis responded that when he held the title, he went on what people called a "bum of the month" tour as he defended his title every month. Ali asked Louis if he was calling him a bum. Louis responded, "you woulda been on the tour." But on this night, as Louis was to discover, he wasn't fighting a bum.

The bell rang, starting the fight, and Conn, as usual, started slowly, even slipping to the canvas while avoiding a punch from Louis. During round two, Louis was again the aggressor as he attacked his smaller opponent to wear him out. Then in the third round, things began to turn around as Conn got the better of the heavyweight champ. By the end of round nine, a confident Conn told Louis that on this night, he was in a fight, and the champ agreed. By the end of round twelve, Conn was clearly in control of the fight. All he had to do was continue to box Louis for the remaining three rounds, and the heavyweight championship would be his. In his corner between rounds, Conn predicted he would knock Lois out in the 13th. His handlers responded by telling him to keep boxing and stay away from the champ. In their view, the fight had already been won. Across the ring, in Louis's corner, his people were telling the champ that he needed a knockout to win.

Conn later said that he had promised his mother (who was then lying on her deathbed in Pittsburgh) that he would win this fight by knocking out Louis. Conn answered the bell for round thirteen and went aggressively after Louis. He was playing into the champ's hands, and Louis took advantage, rocking Conn with a powerful right hand to the jaw. Conn's legs buckled, but he didn't go down. Louis moved in, landing several consecutive punches until Conn did hit the canvas. He was counted out with two seconds left in the round, and Louis had retained his title. After the fight, Conn said, "What's the sense of being Irish if you can't be dumb?" Years later, Conn would ask Louis why he couldn't have just let him be the champion for a few months. Louis responded by telling him he had been champion for twelve rounds but that he couldn't hold the title.

Despite the loss, Conn became a nationwide hero. He did tons of radio interviews and was featured in numerous magazines. He even made a movie that was appropriately titled *The Pittsburgh Kid*. Many fight fans and ring experts believed the bout to have been the greatest fight in history, and the public wanted a rematch. Louis agreed to fight Conn again,

Joe Louis knocks out Billy Conn in 1946.

and the two were scheduled to meet in November of 1942. The fight was set even though both men were heading into the military.

Jimmy Smith may have failed at stopping Conn from marrying his daughter, but he was about to play a major role in stopping the Louis-Conn rematch. In May of 1942, Conn was home on leave to attend the baptism of his son Timmy. Timmy's godfather was Art Rooney, the owner of the Pittsburgh Steelers. Rooney arranged a party at Conn's house and invited Jimmy Smith. Rooney told Conn that his father in law was ready to make peace with him. Rooney had miscalculated the bad blood between the two. It began with Smith verbally attacking Conn, and it ended in a full-fledged fistfight. During the fight, Conn caught Smith on the top of the head with a left; the punch landed, but Conn broke his hand. The rematch was called off due to the injury. Conn and Louis did fight again in 1946, but by that time, Conn was well past his prime, and Louis took him in eight rounds. Conn retired as a fighter in 1948.

When Conn was 73 years old in 1990, he stepped into a Pittsburgh convenience store where a robbery was underway. The Pittsburgh Kid

The grave site of one the greatest light heavyweight
champions in the history of boxing.

didn't hesitate as he floored the robber with one punch and then began wrestling him. The robber got away but not before Conn had pulled off his coat, which contained the man's name and address, and that led to an easy arrest.

Conn passed away in 1993 at the age of 75. He was laid to rest at Calvary Catholic Cemetery in Pittsburgh. Conn is remembered as one of the greatest light heavyweights in boxing history. He is a member of both the Ring Boxing Hall of Fame and the International Boxing Hall of Fame.

If You Go:

There are plenty of other sites in Calvary Catholic Cemetery including the great entertainer Frank Gorshin (see *Keystone Tombstones Volume One*, Chapter 10), former Pennsylvania Governor David Lawrence (see *Keystone Tombstones Volume One*, Chapter 15), and the quarterback of the Four Horsemen of Notre Dame, Harry Stuhldreher (see *Keystone Tombstones Volume One*, Chapter 6). Also, Pittsburgh is loaded with great eateries and taverns. We would recommend you check out Winghart's located at 5 Market Square. We both agreed that this place had the best burgers we had ever tasted. The staff was friendly, and the service was great. The city has a great zoo and is home to Kennywood Park.

6.

JIM CROCE

"You Don't Mess Around with Jim"

County: Chester • Town: Frazer
Buried at Haym Salomon Memorial Park
200 Moores Road

On September 20, 1973, a small commercial airplane took off from Natchitoches Regional Airport in Louisiana. The plane did not gain the necessary altitude to clear a tree at the end of the runway. All five passengers died as a result of the crash. Among them was the 30-year-old singer-songwriter Jim Croce.

Croce was born in Philadelphia on January 10, 1943. He developed an interest in music at a young age. When he was five, he was belting out the song "Lady of Spain" on an accordion. He attended Upper Darby High School, where he would later become the first graduate named to the school's Wall of Fame. After graduation, he enrolled at Villanova University in 1961. During his time at the university, he became a member of the Villanova Singers, and he also worked as a student disc jockey.

For Croce, music had always been a hobby, but now he began to view it more seriously. He formed several college bands and performed at frat parties, coffee houses, and other universities in the Philadelphia area. He later said that his bands played anything the people wanted to hear: "blues, rock, a cappella, railroad music, anything." It was during this time that he met his future wife, Ingrid Jacobson, while he was judging a contest during a hootenanny being held at the Philadelphia Convention Hall. After they married, he converted to his wife's religion, Judaism.

Jim Croce

Beginning in the mid-sixties, Croce began performing with his wife as a duo. They started out covering other artists' songs but soon found themselves enlarging their repertoire to include their compositions. According to Croce, during this time, he would put together a setlist pulled from over 3,000 songs he had learned. Croce later recalled playing some pretty tough bars during this period, saying, "I can still get my guitar off faster than anyone else."

In 1968 Croce and his wife moved to New York City after being encouraged to do so by a record producer named Tommy West. It was in New York where they recorded their first album titled *Jim & Ingrid Croce*. Following the album's release, the couple spent two years on the road to promote it. The Croces hit the college circuit and played small clubs along the way. In all, they would travel over 300,000 miles. Despite their efforts, the album was not a commercial success.

Perhaps because their record failed to do well, the Croces grew weary of the music business and New York City. They sold every guitar they owned, save one, and moved back to the Philadelphia area. Croce worked construction jobs and as a truck driver to pay the bills. At the same time, he continued to write songs based on people he was meeting in truck stops and at local bars.

While at Villanova, Croce had befriended a man by the name of Joe Salviuolo, who was now a record producer. In 1970 Salviuolo introduced Croce to Maury Muehleisen (who would also perish in the 1973 crash), a classically trained guitarist who was also a singer-songwriter. The two began performing together, with Croce backing Muehleisen. Gradually these roles reversed as they discovered that Muehleisen's guitar leads were the ideal accompaniment to Croce's songs.

In 1972 Croce signed a record deal with ABC records. That year he released two albums, *You Don't Mess Around with Jim* and *Life & Times*. The first release was an instant smash. The title song and the song "Operator" both became highly successful singles. Suddenly Croce became a top bill concert performer. He was a very open and friendly performer who welcomed his fans backstage after a concert. Rather than listening to critics, he was always anxious to hear from those in the audience as to what they thought of his performance. For those of you who have never seen Croce perform, there are numerous clips of him on YouTube.

The song "Bad, Bad Leroy Brown" was pulled from *Life & Times* and released as a single. It rocketed up the record charts, reaching number 1 in the summer of 1973 and selling two million copies. Croce's career was booming.

Croce finished recording his third album *I Got a Name* in September of 1973 about one week before his death. The album was released on December 1, 1973. *I Got a Name* proved to be another big hit, and it produced three hit singles: the title song, "Workin' at the Car Wash Blues," and "I'll Have to Say I Love You in a Song." Croce's untimely

*The final resting place of a great singer and songwriter
who left us too soon.*

death also sparked a renewed interest in his earlier work. The song "Time
in a Bottle," which appeared on his first album released the previous year,
reached number one on December 29, 1973. *Photographs and Memories*,
a greatest hits package, was released in 1974 and proved to be a big success. To this day, Croce's music receives a great deal of radio airplay. In
1990 Croce was inducted into the Songwriters Hall of Fame.

Investigators of the crash that took Croce's life determined that it
was due to pilot error. Some believe that the pilot, who had severe coro-
nary artery disease, may have suffered a heart attack during the takeoff.
Although Croce had recently relocated to California, he was laid to rest
in Pennsylvania in the Haym Salomon Cemetery. Croce's wife Ingrid
opened Croce's Restaurant and Jazz Bar in San Diego in 1985. That business is still in operation. The Croce's had one son, Adrian James Croce
(while still unborn, he inspired the song "Time in a Bottle"), who is
an accomplished singer-songwriter. He performs under the name A. J.
Croce and has released multiple CDs.

If You Go:

Should you decide to visit Croce, you are within easy driving distance of Philadelphia. There are numerous things to do in the city, including making visits to grave sites covered in *Keystone Tombstones Volume One* as well as in this volume. The cemetery where Croce was laid to rest is named after Haym Salomon, who was a key figure during the American Revolution. Salomon was a Jewish banker who provided funds to pay for troops, as well as furnish them with food and arms. The Revolution succeeded because he and a few others like him believed in the cause and were willing to fund the effort. Salomon is buried in the Mikveh Israel Cemetery, located on 8th and Spruce Streets in Philadelphia.

This is the grave of Haym Salomon a man who was key in financing the American Revolution.

7.

SAINT KATHARINE DREXEL
AND
SAINT JOHN NEUMANN

"Philadelphia Saints"

Counties: Bucks and Philadelphia • Towns: Bensalem and Philadelphia
Drexel is buried at Saint Katherine Drexel Mission Center and Shrine
1663 Bristol Pike, Bensalem
Neumann is buried at Saint Peter of the Apostle Church
1019 North Fifth Street, Philadelphia

Becoming a saint in the Catholic Church is no easy task. First, when a person is considered for sainthood, a bishop is given the job of investigating that person's life. If the bishop concludes that further consideration is warranted, the person is declared a servant of God. Then a church official acts as an advocate for the candidate and attempts to prove that the candidate lived a heroic and virtuous life. The advocate collects documents and testimony that are then presented to the Congregation for the Causes of Saints in Rome. If approved, the candidate gets a new title, "Venerable." Next, a miracle must occur through the intercession of the candidate and said miracle must be confirmed generally by the Roman Medical Board. Once confirmed, the candidate earns the title "Blessed." Unless waived by the pope, a second miracle is required before the Pope declares the candidate a saint. Two saints lie in rest in the Philadelphia area, Saint Katharine Drexel and Saint John Neumann.

Katharine Drexel was born in Philadelphia on November 26, 1858. Her family was very well-to-do as they possessed a considerable banking fortune. Her uncle Anthony founded Drexel University in Philadelphia. Drexel had two sisters: Louise and Elizabeth. In 1887, the three sisters

Saint Katherine Drexel

traveled to Rome. Due to the recent deaths of their parents, they had inherited the family fortune. On January 27th, they assisted at a private mass celebrated by Pope Leo XIII; later, they would have a private audience with him. After the audience, Katherine asked the pontiff if he could spare a few minutes to speak with her privately, and he granted her wish. She pleaded with the pope to send Catholic missionaries to work with American Indians. Leo responded, "Why not, my child, yourself become a missionary." He gave Drexel his blessing, and the audience ended.

In 1874, the Catholic Church in America established the Bureau of Catholic Indian Missions. It is still in existence. Upon its founding its purpose was stated as:

To direct the administration of those agencies as were assigned to the care of Catholic missionaries.

To secure, if possible, the remainder of those agencies to which Catholic missionaries were justly entitled under the terms of the peace policy.

To protect the religious faith and material interests of all Catholic Indians.

To secure the establishment of suitable schools for Indian boys and girls.

To secure for the Indians moral and practical Christian teachers with adequate compensation for their services and to develop a general interest in Indian education.

To secure means to erect school buildings, in all cases possible.

Drexel wholeheartedly supported and contributed to the bureau.

Drexel resolved to use her wealth to aid both Indian and African Americans. In 1885 she established a school for Native Americans in Santa Fe, New Mexico. In 1889 she decided to become a nun and started her training with the Sisters of Mercy in Pittsburgh. Two years later, she founded her order of nuns: The Sisters of the Blessed Sacrament for Indians and Colored People. The title contained the purpose of the new order to bring the Blessed Sacrament to the two races. Using her vast wealth, she founded and financed over sixty missions and schools throughout the United States. She is also credited with founding the only historically African American Roman Catholic University in the nation, Xavier University, which is in Louisiana.

Here is the tomb of Saint Katherine Drexel.

In 1935 Drexel suffered a heart attack, and two years later, she gave up the office of the superior general. She continued her devotion to the Eucharist, and to the two races her order was established to help. She died at the age of 96 on March 3, 1955.

As detailed at the beginning of this chapter, becoming a Catholic saint is not easy, and it generally takes a very long time to be canonized after one's death. For example, the only other American-born Catholic saint, Elizabeth Ann Seton, died in 1821 and was not declared a saint until 1975. In Drexel's case, during her lifetime, people were already calling her a saint, and these people included bishops and archbishops. Bishop Joseph McShea, who preached at her funeral, said, "I think she was a saint. I am convinced she was a saint and have no knowledge of any other dedicated woman, lay or religious, no personal knowledge, that would exceed her in sanctity."

There was still the need for miracles before Drexel could be named a saint. George and Bea Gutherman lived in Bensalem, where they raised a family that included eleven children. In 1974 one of their sons named Bob was hospitalized with a very serious ear infection. The infection was life-threatening, and even if the boy survived, he was expected to lose his hearing. The family prayed directly to Drexel for help, and their son's fever disappeared as did the infection. Also, the documented inner ear damage healed. In 1987 the Roman medical board declared the case to be a miracle and attributed the cure to Drexel. In 1994 the story of a young girl named Amanda Wall provided the second miracle. Wall had been born deaf, but after family and friends prayed directly to Drexel, she was able to hear. In 2000 the church found that Wall's cure was due to the intercession of Drexel. As a result, Drexel was canonized on October 1, 2000. Her feast day is celebrated on March 3, the anniversary of her death. Her body lies under the main altar in Saint Elizabeth Chapel, which is part of the Saint Katharine Drexel Mission Center and National Shrine.

John Neumann was born on March 28, 1811, in Prachatitz, Bohemia. He began his education at the village school when he was six years of age. From the beginning, it was clear that he was both intelligent and eager to learn. He grew to love the natural sciences and studied intently in that area. He also showed his spiritual side at a young age, becoming an altar boy at the age of ten.

Neumann entered the seminary in 1831. He had a driving ambition to become a priest. By 1835 he had passed the examination making him eligible to receive Holy Orders, the catholic sacrament one receives upon entering the priesthood. Unfortunately for Neumann, his bishop had decided that at present, there would be no ordinations as Bohemia already had more than enough priests.

By this time, Neumann could speak eight languages, including English. Neumann decided he would go to America, where there was a need for priests and missionaries who spoke German. He arrived in America with the hope of being ordained. He met with Bishop John Dubois, who then governed the Diocese of New York. The bishop oversaw a huge territory that included all of New York and New Jersey. Neumann must have made the right impression because he was ordained on June 25, 1836, in the old Saint Patrick's Cathedral on Mott Street in New York City.

Bishop Dubois sent Neumann to work with German immigrants in the area of Niagara Falls. His parish contained about 400 Catholics that lived in an area covering nine hundred square miles. At the time, most of the area would have been described as the frontier. He began traveling the countryside by horse to minister to his flock. He would visit the sick, teach catechism to children, and train others to teach it when he

Saint John Neumann

left. Several churches were built, including Saint Peter and Paul Catholic Church in Williamsville, New York. Neumann founded this church and served as its pastor for four years.

By 1840 Neumann came to believe that the spiritual direction he required could only be supplied by an established religious order.

After receiving permission from Bishop Dubois, Neumann joined the Redemptorist Fathers in Pittsburgh. In 1842 he took his vows in Baltimore, Maryland, and became a full member of this congregation. He was then stationed at Saint James Church in Baltimore, but he continued his practice of traveling long distances to minister to German settlers. In 1847 he was appointed Provincial Superior of the United States Redemptorists. On February 10, 1848, Neumann became a United States citizen. At this point, he was stationed at Saint Alphonsus Church in Baltimore, where he wrote catechisms in both German and English.

In 1852 Pope Pius IX appointed Neumann to the post of Bishop of Philadelphia. At the time of his appointment, Philadelphia was the largest Diocese in the United States. As was his practice, Neumann frequently traveled to visit parishes scattered throughout the large area he now headed. He became the first bishop in the country to establish a Catholic school system. This system became the model for the parochial school system. New churches were built at an ever-quickening pace. As a matter of fact, during his first three years as a bishop, a new church was opened each month. His programs were popular throughout the diocese, and he became known as the "Little Bishop."

In 1854 Neumann traveled to Rome at the invitation of the Pope. He was present on December 8th when Pope Pius IX issued his declaration of the Dogma of the Immaculate Conception. He took advantage of this trip to Europe to visit his father, who he had not seen in 28 years. Upon his return to Philadelphia, Neumann founded a new order of nuns: The Sisters of Saint Francis, who dedicated themselves to teaching and nursing. Neumann had a history of using nuns to spread the faith. Back in 1847, he had welcomed a group of nuns from Munich known as the School Sisters of Notre Dame to America. He provided them with teaching assignments in Philadelphia, New York, Pittsburgh, and Baltimore.

On January 5, 1860, while running errands, Neumann suffered a stroke, collapsed, and died on a city street in Philadelphia. He was only 49 years old. In those 49 years, he had established 80 churches and contributed to the establishment of ten orders of nuns.

Despite all his good work, the need for miracles that could be attributed to Neumann remained. On July 8, 1949, J. Kent Lenahan was

Monument in Philadelphia honoring
Saint John Neumann.

crushed between a car and a utility pole as a result of an automobile accident. His skull was crushed, and while in the hospital, his fever rose to 107 degrees. There was little hope that he would recover. His parents obtained a piece of a cassock that had been worn by Neumann. They placed the piece on their son, and within a few hours, his temperature dropped to 100 degrees. Also, his injuries began to heal. Five weeks later, he walked out of the hospital without assistance. The church declared his recovery a miracle and gave the credit for it to Neumann.

Michael Flanigan was six years old in 1963 when it was discovered that he had Ewing's Sarcoma, a lethal form of bone cancer. The doctors gave the boy six months to live. His parents began taking the boy to Neumann's shrine, and after several visits, the boy began to recover. By Christmas of 1963, all signs of cancer had vanished. In 1975 the church declared Michael's cure a miracle and attributed it to the intercession of Neumann. As a result, Neumann was canonized in 1977 by Pope Paul VI.

Neumann was buried unembalmed in a wooden casket beneath the floor of Saint Peter of the Apostle Church. His body was exhumed in 1902 so that the required inspections for sainthood could be completed.

Final resting place of Saint John Neumann beneath an alter at Saint Peter of the Apostle Church in Philadelphia.

His remains at the time were found to be intact, and after the inspection, the body was returned to the original grave. In 1962 Neumann's body was again exhumed, and a face mask was placed over the skull. The body was then placed in a glass coffin and placed under the altar in the Saint John Neumann Shrine, which had been constructed on the lower level of the Saint Peter of the Apostle Church.

If You Go:

Keystone Tombstones Volume One contains stories of famous people buried in the Philadelphia area, including Benjamin Franklin, William Anderson, Harry Kalas, Frank Rizzo, and Bill Tilden. Should you make the trip, you might want to pick that volume up and visit some of those graves as well. There are plenty of Philadelphia gravesites in this volume as well, including Richie Ashburn, John Wanamaker, Bessie Smith, Bert Bell, and in the chapter titled "Philadelphia's Sinners," several reputed mafia figures are profiled. Philadelphia is a historical Mecca, and you can find plenty to do there, including making visits to Independence Hall and the Constitution Center. There are numerous great places throughout the city where one can stop for refreshments.

8.

STEPHEN FOSTER

"The Music Man"

County: Allegheny • Town: Pittsburgh
Buried at Allegheny Cemetery
4734 Butler Street

Who is America's greatest songwriter? Some would say Cole Porter, Irving Berlin, Duke Ellington, or the Gershwins. More recent names like Bob Dylan, Bruce Springsteen, Paul Simon, Smokey Robinson, and Carole King would all find supporters. The first great American songwriter would have to be considered, as well. His name was Stephen Foster, and even today, almost 150 years since his death, his songs are still being performed and recorded.

Stephen Foster was born on July 4, 1826, near Pittsburgh. He was the ninth of ten children born to William and Eliza Foster. The Fosters were a middle-class family. As a boy, Foster was privately tutored, and he also attended private academies in Pittsburgh. From the start, Foster showed more interest in music than in other subjects. In 1839, Foster's older brother, William, had started an apprenticeship as an engineer in Towanda. Foster was placed in William's care, and from 1839 to 1841, he attended Athens Academy. It was here that he composed his first song, "Tioga Waltz," which he performed during the school's 1839 graduation ceremony.

In 1846, Foster moved to Cincinnati, Ohio, where he worked as a bookkeeper for a steamship company. It was in Ohio where Foster composed his first successful songs, including "Oh! Susanna." By 1850 Foster had published the music to twelve songs. That same year, he returned to Pittsburgh, where he married Jane Denny MacDowell. It wasn't until

Stephen Foster

1852 that the couple went on their honeymoon to New Orleans. It was Foster's only trip to the deep South.

By this time, Foster had decided to become a professional composer. He was influenced by Henry Kleber, a German immigrant, who instructed Foster in both composition and songwriting. Foster signed a contract with the Christy Minstrels. The Minstrels were a blackface group formed by the then famous ballad singer Edwin Pearce Christy. The centerpiece of the group's performances became Foster's songs. Foster was writing some of his most famous songs during this period, including "Camptown

OH! SUSANNA.

Races," "My Old Kentucky Home," and "Old Folks at Home," which is also known as "Swanee River." Christy paid Foster $15,000 for the exclusive rights to "Old Folks at Home."

In 1853 Foster moved close to New York to be nearer to his music publishers. His wife joined him a year later. The couple returned to Pittsburgh in the later part of 1854. They lived with Foster's parents for a time, but both his mother and father passed away in 1855. After their deaths, Foster and his wife lived in multiple boarding houses.

Foster's attempt to make a living as a songwriter was unique for the times. Copyright laws regarding music were quite limited. Foster received very little in royalties for most of his work. For example, he was paid $100 for "Oh Susanna." Also, publishers with whom he had no connection would print his songs and pay him nothing. In today's music business, Foster would be making millions.

In 1860 Foster moved back to New York City. His marriage had always been rocky, and a year later, his wife left him and returned to Pittsburgh. By 1863 he began writing songs with George Cooper. Foster supplied the music, and Cooper contributed lyrics designed to appeal to musical theater audiences. Foster's fortunes failed to improve with the new partnership. By 1864 Foster was living in the North American Hotel in the Bowery section of New York. Early that year, he developed a fever that confined him to his bed for several days. He got up to call a chambermaid and fell, hitting the washbasin next to his bed and injuring his head. Foster was taken to the Bellevue Hospital, where he died three days later, on January 13th. He was just 37 years old. His wallet at the time of his death contained 38 cents in Civil War script, three pennies, and a note that read "dear friends and gentle hearts." One of his great works, "Beautiful Dreamer," was published after his death.

In 1970, Foster was inducted into the Songwriters Hall of Fame. He is also a member of the Nashville Songwriters Hall of Fame. "My Old Kentucky Home" is the official state song of Kentucky, and it is sung every year as the horses enter the track at Churchill Downs for the running of the Kentucky Derby. In the 1990s, Bob Dylan recorded the Foster composition "Hard Times" for his album *Good as I've Been to You*. Bruce Springsteen has performed the same song in concert. In 2005, eighteen of Foster's songs were recorded for the album *Beautiful Dreamer: The Songs of Stephen Foster*. The artists who recorded the songs included John Prine, Roger McGuinn, and Allison Krauss. The record won the Grammy for Best Traditional Folk Album.

There are many memorials to Foster. Chief among these is the Stephen Foster Memorial on the campus of the University of Pittsburgh. The building houses the Stephen Foster Memorial Museum, which contains the largest collection of Foster's songs, recordings, and memorabilia. A lake at Mount Pisgah State Park in Pennsylvania is named in his honor. In Cincinnati, there is a statue of Foster overlooking the Ohio River. During the first weekend in July, the Lawrenceville Historical Society and the Allegheny Cemetery Historical Association host the Stephen Foster Music and Heritage Festival appropriately called Doo Dah Days.

If You Go:

Allegheny Cemetery is a historical treasure. Besides Foster, there are many notable interments. The famed singer and actress Lillian Russell was laid to rest here. Hall of Fame baseball player Josh Gibson (see Chapter 9), who hit 800 home runs in a 17-year career, is buried in Allegheny Cemetery.

The gravesite of America's first great songwriter.

Gibson was a major star in the Negro League, and many who saw him play claimed he was as good if not better than Babe Ruth. Henry Thaw, the man who shot and killed the noted architect Stanford White on the roof of Madison Square Garden, is here as well. The murder is part of the hit movie *Ragtime*. The great jazz saxophonist Stanley Turrentine's final resting place is in Allegheny Cemetery.

Two Civil War Medal of Honor recipients, Archibald H. Rowand Jr. and Alfred L. Pearson, are buried here as well. After the war, Pearson commanded the National Guardsmen who were sent to Luzerne County to quell riots in the Coal Region. He ordered his men to open fire on the rioters and killed several of them. As a result, he was arrested and charged with murder, but a grand jury failed to indict him, and he was set free.

Also, you may want to visit the Arsenal Monument on the cemetery's grounds. The monument honors 43 women buried here after an explosion at the nearby Allegheny Arsenal took their lives. The explosion was the worst industrial accident associated with the Civil War.

Not far from the cemetery, there is a great restaurant called Piccolo Forno. It is located at 3801 Butler Street. The eatery offers great service and terrific Italian food that is very reasonably priced. It's worth checking out.

9.

JOSH GIBSON
"The Black Babe Ruth"

County: Allegheny • Town: Pittsburgh
Buried at Allegheny Cemetery
Address: 4734 Butler Street

Josh Gibson is generally considered the greatest hitter in the history of black baseball. An almost mythical figure, Gibson was often referred to as the "Black Babe Ruth" due to his tremendous power at the plate. Those who followed Negro League baseball regularly preferred to think of Ruth as the "White Josh Gibson." Statistical validation for Negro League players is difficult, but Gibson reportedly won nine home run titles and four batting championships during a seventeen-year career that began in 1930 and ended in 1946. The Baseball Hall of Fame claims he hit "almost 800" homers in that span against Negro League and independent baseball opposition. They report his lifetime batting average to be .359, and he has been credited with as many as 84 homers in one season. Belting home runs of more than 500 feet was not unusual for Gibson. One homer in Monessen, Pennsylvania, was measured at 575 feet, and one in a Negro League game in Yankee Stadium measured 580 feet. Although never proven, infielder Jack Marshall of the Chicago American Giants and others claimed they saw Gibson hit a fair ball out of Yankee Stadium. If so, it would be the only fair ball ever hit out of the House that Ruth Built.

Born in Buena Vista, Georgia, on December 21, 1911, Joshua Gibson moved to Pittsburgh in 1923 after his father found work at a Pittsburgh steel company. He initially planned to become an electrician and attended two vocational schools. However, he began to entertain thoughts of a baseball career at the age of sixteen after a job as an elevator operator

Josh Gibson

at Gimbels department store led to a spot on an amateur team sponsored by Gimbels. His professional career began at the age of eighteen under unusual circumstances. The Homestead Grays were playing the Kansas

City Monarchs in Pittsburgh on July 31, 1930, and the Grays' catcher injured his hand and was unable to continue. The Grays' manager Julius "Judy" Johnson knew of Gibson's reputation as a semi-pro player for the Pittsburgh Crawfords and had seen him in the crowd. Johnson went into the stands, found Gibson, and asked if he wanted to catch. He said, "Yes, sir." They held up the game while he put on a uniform. He played so well they signed him the next day.

In 1928, Josh Gibson met Helen Mason, and the two married in March 1929. Helen was pregnant when Gibson made his debut with the Grays. A few days later, on August 11, Helen went into premature labor and died while giving birth to twins, a son Joshua and a daughter named Helen.

Gibson played for the Grays the rest of that season and in 1931, before jumping to the Crawfords from 1932 to 1936. He caught Satchel Paige in 1936 to form the most popular battery in African American history. He returned to the Grays from 1937 to 1939 and from 1942 to 1946. He started 1937 in the Dominican Republic and played in Mexico from 1940 to 1941.

The thing that makes his statistics so difficult to analyze is that Negro League statistics are extremely sketchy, and the level of their reliability is further compromised by the fact that they are generally intermingled with figures compiled in games played against other levels of competition. The Negro Leagues generally found it more profitable to schedule relatively few league games, allowing the teams to earn extra money through barnstorming against semi-pro and other non-league teams.

Splitting most of his career between the Negro Leagues' two most dominant teams, the Homestead Grays and the Pittsburgh Crawfords, Gibson is estimated to have hit close to 800 home runs over his seventeen-year playing career. His lifetime batting average was somewhere between .359 and .384, and he batted over .400 at least twice. He hit .351 in 56 at-bats in exhibition games played against white major leaguers.

Satchel Paige called him "the greatest hitter who ever lived" and Monte Irvin, who played against Gibson in the Negro Leagues and later

Josh Gibson scores a run in the 1944 Negro League East-West All-Star Game at Comiskey Park

with Willie Mays on the New York Giants said, "I played with Willie Mays and against Hank Aaron. They were tremendous players, but they were no Josh Gibson. He had an eye like Ted Williams and the power of Babe Ruth."

While Gibson certainly could have helped any major league team, the unwritten rules of baseball kept him out of the majors his entire career.

In early 1943, Josh Gibson fell into a coma and was diagnosed with a brain tumor. He came out of the coma but refused the option of surgical removal. He lived and played the next four years with recurring head-aches. He died of a stroke in 1947 at the age of 35, just three months before Jackie Robinson became the first black player in modern major league history. He was buried in the Allegheny Cemetery, where he lay in an unmarked grave for nearly thirty years. His teammate Ted Page started a movement in 1975 to obtain a marker for Josh Gibson. Pirates legend Willie Stargell donated the first $100, and Bowie Kuhn, then Major League Baseball Commissioner, donated most of the rest. It reads "Josh Gibson, 1911–1947, Legendary Baseball Player."

In 1972, Gibson and teammate Buck Leonard were the second and third players, behind Satchel Paige, to be inducted into the Baseball Hall of Fame for their performance in the Negro Leagues.

There are many stories about Josh Gibson's baseball feats, but one of the most popular is told in Robert W. Peterson's book *Only the Ball Was White* . . .

One day during the 1930s, the Pittsburgh Crawfords were playing at Forbes Field in Pittsburgh, where their young catcher, Josh Gibson, hit the ball so high and so far that no one saw it come down. After scanning the sky carefully for a few minutes, the umpire deliberated and ruled it a home run. The next day the Crawfords were playing in Philadelphia when suddenly a ball dropped out of the heavens and was caught by the startled center fielder on the opposing club. The umpire made the only possible ruling. Pointing to Gibson, he shouted, "Yer out— yesterday in Pittsburgh!"

This modest tombstone pays tribute to the man many consider to be the greatest hitter in the history of baseball.

If You Go:

Allegheny Cemetery is a well-maintained, large, historic cemetery with a great number of interesting graves. Near Josh Gibson's grave is the grave of colorful, controversial William "Gus" Greenlee. Greenlee migrated to Pittsburgh from North Carolina in 1916. He established a bootlegging business that he operated from his taxi, and he and a friend are credited with introducing the numbers racket to Pittsburgh in 1926. He and William Harris turned it into one of the largest and most complex gambling networks of the period. He opened a nightclub called The Crawford Grill and attracted numerous jazz greats, including Louis Armstrong, Dizzy Gillespie, and Miles Davis. "The Grill" was a center of black life in Pittsburgh's Hill District. He was very involved in boxing as a manager and was known for his many charitable acts and contributions. He was perhaps best known, however, as the owner of the Pittsburgh Crawfords baseball team from 1931 to 1939. The 1935 squad may have been the best to play in the Negro League, as it fielded five Baseball Hall of Fame players, including Josh Gibson, Satchel Paige, Oscar Charleston, Judy Johnson, and Cool Papa Bell. He was also president of the Negro National League for five years and helped institute the famous East-West Game, an all-star baseball game played in Chicago. He died of a stroke in 1952.

Two of Josh Gibson's teammates, Harold Tinker and Theodore "Ted" Page, are also buried in Allegheny Cemetery as is Albert "Rosey" Roswell, a broadcaster and "voice of the Pittsburgh Pirates" for nineteen seasons. He was one of the first broadcasters to enthusiastically and unabashedly cheer on the air. His famous trademark was his home run call, "Raise the window, Aunt Minnie!" followed by his partner dropping a tray filled with nuts and bolts, simulating the sound of broken glass.

Also buried there are Stephen Foster (see Chapter 8), Lillian Russell, Harry Thaw (see Chapter 24), General John Neville of Whiskey Rebellion fame, two Congressional Medal of Honor recipients (see the chapter on Stephen Foster), and many other historical figures.

10.

WINFIELD SCOTT HANCOCK
"Hancock the Superb"

County: Montgomery • Town: Norristown
Buried at Montgomery Cemetery
1 Hartranft Avenue

Winfield Scott Hancock was an American hero named after an American hero and given an appropriate and well-earned nickname, "Hancock the Superb." He was a career U.S. Army Officer, a hero in the Civil War, a commanding general at the Battle of Gettysburg, and the Democratic nominee for president in 1880.

Winfield Scott Hancock was born in Montgomery County, Pennsylvania, on Valentine's Day in 1824. He was named after General Winfield Scott, a hero in the War of 1812. Hancock was born with an identical twin brother named Hilary Booker Hancock. Hancock was educated at Norristown Academy at first but transferred to public schools in the late 1830s. In 1840, he was nominated to West Point by Congressman Joseph Fornance. He graduated in 1844, ranked eighteenth of twenty-five. He was commissioned a second lieutenant and assigned to the infantry.

When the Mexican War broke out in 1846, he was initially assigned to recruiting in Kentucky. He worked hard to get assigned to the front, but he was so successful as a recruiter, they were reluctant to let him go. He finally did get assigned to the front in July of 1847 in a regiment that made up part of the army led by General Winfield Scott. He was promoted to 1st lieutenant for "gallant and meritorious conduct" at the Battle of Churubusco, where he was wounded in the knee and developed a fever. The fever kept him from participating in the final breakthrough

Winfield Scott Hancock

at Mexico City much to his regret. He remained in Mexico until the peace treaty was signed in 1848.

After the Mexican War, he served in the West, in Florida, and elsewhere. It was while serving in St. Louis that he met Almira (Allie) Russell, whom he married in 1850. The couple had two children, Russell (1850–1884) and Ada (1857–1875). In 1855, he was promoted to captain, and in November 1858, he was stationed in southern California and joined by Almira and the children. There, Hancock became friends with several officers from the South and became especially close to Lewis Armistead of Virginia. At the outbreak of the Civil War, Armistead and other Southerners were leaving to join the Confederate Army, while Hancock was remaining in the U.S. Army.

On June 15, 1861, Hancock and Almira hosted a party for their friends who were scattered because of the war. The party has become a legend and is recounted in Michael Shaara's *The Killer Angels* and the movie *Gettysburg*. Armistead, who was widowed twice, had grown very close to the Hancocks and shed tears when it became time to end the party and depart. He gave some personal effects to Almira for safekeeping and promised he would not take arms against his friend, "Winnie."

Almira said later that at the Battle of Gettysburg, Hancock's men killed three of the six Confederates who attended that party.

Hancock headed east to assume quartermaster duties for a rapidly growing army, but on September 23, 1861, he was promoted to brigadier general and given command of an infantry brigade in the Amy of the Potomac. He took part in the Peninsula Campaign, and at the Battle of Williamsburg on May 5, 1862, he handled his troop so well that General George McClellan reported: "Hancock was superb." The epithet seemed to stick to him afterward, and "Hancock the Superb" was born.

He played a significant role at the Battle of Antietam and shortly afterward was promoted to Major General

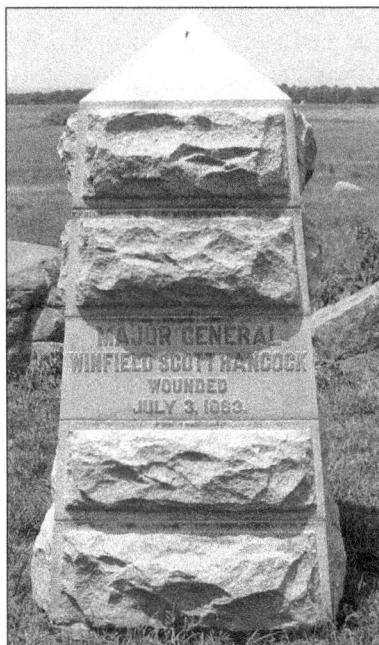

This monument marks the spot at Gettysburg where Hancock was wounded. The bullet that was removed from Hancock is preserved by the Montgomery County Historical Society.

of Volunteers in November 1862. He led his division in the disastrous attack on Marye's Heights in the Battle of Fredericksburg the following month, where he was wounded in the abdomen. He was wounded again at the Battle of Chancellorsville, covering General Hooker's withdrawal. On that day, General Darius Couch asked to be transferred out of the Army of the Potomac in protest of the actions of General Hooker. As a result, Hancock assumed command of 11 Corps, which he would lead until shortly before the war's end (General Couch had a long distinguished military career and has the remains of a fortification built to defend Harrisburg named after him in Lemoyne, Pennsylvania.).

Hancock's most famous service was at the Battle of Gettysburg during July 1-3, 1863. On the first day, after his friend Maj. Gen. John Reynolds (see *Keystone Tombstones Volume One,* Chapter 24) was killed, Gen. George Meade (see *Keystone Tombstones Volume One*, Chapter 20), the new commander of the Army of the Potomac, sent Hancock ahead to take command and to decide whether to continue to fight there or to fall back. He decided to stay, rallied his troops, and held Cemetery Ridge until the arrival of the main body of the Federal Army. During the second day's battle, he commanded the left-center and, after General Sickles had been wounded, the whole left wing. On the third day, he commanded the left-center and thus bore the brunt of Pickett's Charge. Hancock was shot in the groin while rallying and commanding his troops on horseback. Although severely wounded, he refused to be evacuated to the rear until the battle was resolved. During the battle, his old friend General Lewis Armistead was mortally wounded. As he lay dying, he asked to see Hancock. When told that Hancock could not come to see him because he had been wounded himself, Armistead asked that Hancock be told that he was sorry. Armistead died two days later, while Hancock took six months to recover enough to return to command. There is a monument on the Gettysburg Battlefield commemorating their friendship and another marking the spot where Armistead fell. Hancock was considered by many to have made the most impact by a general at Gettysburg. His courage in the face of fire and leadership played a huge role in the Union victory.

This is the Friend to Friend monument in the Gettysburg National Cemetery. The monument portrays the final moments in the life of Confederate General Lewis Armistead who died at Gettysburg and was close friends with General Hancock.

This monument on the Gettysburg battlefield marks the spot where Confederate General Lewis Armistead fell mortally wounded.

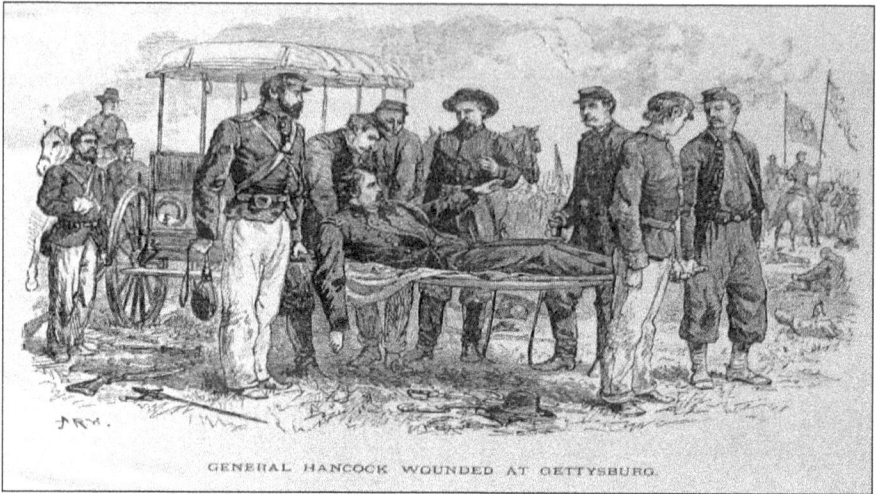

GENERAL HANCOCK WOUNDED AT GETTYSBURG.

This drawing of a wounded Hancock at Gettysburg is in the office at the Montgomery Cemetery.

Hancock suffered from the effects of his Gettysburg wound for the rest of the war. After recuperating in Norristown, he returned in March to the front and led his old corps under General Ulysses S. Grant in the 1864 Overland Campaign but was never quite his old self. He performed well at the Battle of the Wilderness, which began in May, and continued to fight at Yellow Tavern, North Anna, Old Church, Cold Harbor, Trevilian Station, and finally, the siege of Petersburg. In June, his Gettysburg wound reopened, but he soon resumed command, sometimes traveling by ambulance. After his corps participated in the assaults at Deep Bottom, Hancock was promoted to brigadier general in the Regular Army, effective August 12, 1864.

In Grant's campaign against Lee, Hancock and his famed 11 Corps were repeatedly called upon to plunge into the very worst of the fighting, and the casualties were terrible. The losses and lingering effects of his Gettysburg wound caused Hancock to give up field command in November 1864. He left the 11 Corps after a year in which it had suffered over 40,000 casualties but had achieved significant military victories. He was again promoted in March 1865 to brevet major general in the Regular Army.

After the assassination of Abraham Lincoln in April, Hancock was placed in charge of Washington, D.C., and it was under his command that John Wilkes Booth's accomplices were tried and executed. Hancock was reluctant to execute some of the less-culpable conspirators, especially Mary Surratt. He hoped Surratt would receive a pardon from President Johnson. He was so hopeful that he posted messengers from the arsenal, where the hangings took place, to the White House, ready to relay the news of a pardon to him, but no pardon was forthcoming. Afterward, he wrote that "every soldier was bound to act as I did under similar circumstances."

Hancock remained in the postwar army, and in 1866 Grant had him promoted to major general in the Regular Army, and he served at that rank for the rest of his life. He served briefly in the West and then was named military governor of Louisiana during Reconstruction. His policies there angered Republicans and Grant but made him popular among Democrats. When Grant won the presidency in 1868, Hancock found himself transferred to the Department of Dakota, which covered Minnesota, Montana, and the Dakotas. It was during this tour that Hancock contributed to the creation of Yellowstone National Park and had a summit (Mt. Hancock) at the southern boundary named in his honor.

With the death of General George Meade in 1872, Hancock became the senior major general in the U.S. Army and was assigned to take Meade's place as commander of the Division of the Atlantic at Governor's Island in New York Harbor.

Hancock had been considered as a presidential nominee by the Democrats as early as 1864. In 1880, he was finally chosen at the convention in Cincinnati, along with William Hayden English of Indiana as his running mate. They ran against James Garfield and Chester Arthur in an election that was very close in the popular vote, but not so close in the electoral. Garfield won by less than 10,000 votes but won the electoral vote 214 to 155. Garfield was assassinated in September 1881.

Hancock finished his life as Commander of the Division of the Atlantic and died at Governor's Island from an infected carbuncle complicated by diabetes on February 9, 1886. After a funeral in New York City, General Hancock's remains were taken to his boyhood home of Norristown, Pennsylvania, and placed with his daughter Ada in a mausoleum that he had designed.

Winfield Scott Hancock is memorialized three times at Gettysburg: once in a statue on Cemetery Hill, once on a statue as part of the Pennsylvania Memorial, and as a sculpture on the New York State Monument. There are statues in Washington, D.C., at Pennsylvania Avenue and 7th Street N.W. and in Fairmont Park in Philadelphia and a bronze bust in Hancock Square, New York City. His portrait adorns U.S. currency on the $2 silver certificate series of 1886 and is quite valuable today.

Actor Brian Mallon portrayed Hancock in two films about the Civil War: *Gettysburg* (1993) and *Gods and Generals* (2003). He is portrayed very favorably in both films. There are numerous books about Hancock, the most notable is *Winfield Scott Hancock: A Soldier's Life,* written by David M. Jordan and published in 1998.

Here is the grave of one of the greatest Union Civil War generals.

If You Go:
There are a few other interesting graves in Montgomery Cemetery. The most notable is the grave of John Frederick Hartranft, who will be the subject of a chapter in a subsequent volume. Hartranft was awarded the Congressional Medal of Honor for his actions at the first Battle of Manassas. He rose to the rank of brigadier general and, after the war, was appointed a special provost marshall during the trial of those accused in President Lincoln's assassination. He led the convicted parties to the gallows and read them their last rites before they were hanged.

Returning to civilian life, he served as auditor general of Pennsylvania in John White Geary's (see *Keystone Tombstones Volume One*, Chapter 9) administration before being elected governor in 1872. He was governor on the Day of the Rope, June 21, 1877, when ten Molly Maguires were hanged (see *Keystone Tombstones Volume One*, Chapter 13).

Also buried in Montgomery Cemetery with Hancock is Brigadier General Samuel Kosciuszko Zook who fought with him at Gettysburg and was fatally wounded on the second day, and Brigadier General Adam Jacoby Slemmer who ignored pressure by the confederates to surrender his command at Fort Barrancas, Florida in 1861, instead moving it to Fort Pickens, Santa Rosa Island. This move ensured Union control of the Gulf of Mexico throughout the war.

Nearby Montgomery Cemetery at Lower Providence Presbyterian Church Cemetery in Eagleville lies the body of Civil War Congressional Medal of Honor recipient Hillary Beyer. He was awarded his Medal of Honor for his bravery at the Battle of Antietam, Maryland, in September 1862.

We were hungry and thirsty after our visit to Norristown and found a great place just down the road from Lower Providence Presbyterian Church at 3300 Ridge Pike. It's called Brother Paul's and had a great menu and service. You can sit inside or outside and choose from many delicious sounding items on the menu. We both loved our sandwiches. There were many options for wetting your whistle too. While we were waiting for our food, we loved taking in the décor. There were many great photographs throughout the large bar and dining areas. We even got to meet one of the Pauls himself. The Pauls are brothers-in-law, so we found out. He seemed like a fine American, so we asked if he might have us back for a book signing some evening. It looks like a fun place to have a pint or two. We're hoping he says, "yes."

Here are the Joes at Brothers Pauls refreshing ourselves after visiting Montgomery Cemetery. We hope to get back to visit the brothers in the future.

II.

MILTON S. HERSHEY
"The Chocolate King"

County: Dauphin • Town: Hershey
Buried at Hershey Cemetery
On Route 743/Laudermilch Road

Milton Hershey endured years of failure before introducing milk choco-late to the world and then used his fortune to help those less fortunate. He went on to become one of the wealthiest individuals in America whose products are known all over the world. He built a town, which bears his name, and his generosity continues to touch the lives of thousands.

Milton Snavely Hershey was born on a central Pennsylvania farm in Derry Township on September 13, 1857. His education was haphaz-ard and ended after the fourth grade when his father decided he should become an apprentice to a printer in Lancaster. He hated it and was fired. His mother found him a second apprenticeship with a confectioner named Joseph Royer, which he found much more appealing.

After four years, at the age of nineteen, he established his candy-making business in Philadelphia. It was 1876, and he hoped to take advantage of the Great Centennial Exposition, celebrating the 100th anniversary of the Declaration of Independence. He kept it going for six years, but the strain of making taffy and caramels all night and selling them from a pushcart all day eventually wore him down, and he closed shop in 1882.

He moved to Denver and worked for a candy maker and then tried to establish his own candy business in Chicago and then New York, both of which failed.

Milton Hershey

He returned to Lancaster in 1883 and set up yet another candy manufacturing business that specialized in producing caramel. He concentrated on making fine caramels using fresh ingredients, and it worked. Soon his Lancaster Caramel Company was shipping all over the U.S. and Europe and employed 1400 people.

In 1893, Milton Hershey attended the World's Fair in Chicago, which was officially known as the World's Columbian Exposition. He was so impressed with chocolate-making machinery from a German

Milton and Kitty Hershey at the Great Pyramid in Egypt.

exhibitor that he purchased the machinery and began to make chocolate and chocolate-covered caramel products and cocoas as an arm of the Lancaster Caramel Company. At that time, milk chocolate was considered a luxury imported item, but Hershey was fascinated with making chocolate. In 1900 he sold Lancaster Caramel and acquired 200 acres in Derry Township, where he built what was to become the world's largest chocolate-making plant. He created his formula for milk chocolate and, being surrounded by dairy farms, was able to use fresh milk to mass-produce quality milk chocolate.

The Hershey Chocolate Company thrived, and Hershey believed that his company and the community were intertwined and that he had a responsibility to his employees and the community. He directed the development of a town with nice homes, parks, transportation, and recreational facilities, like Hershey Park, which opened in 1907. The town of Hershey now promotes itself as the "sweetest place on Earth."

In 1898 Hershey married Catherine "Kitty" Sweeney, a beautiful Irish Catholic girl from New York. They were very happy together but saddened that they had no children. To fill this void, they founded the Hershey Industrial School, now known as Milton Hershey School, for orphaned boys in 1909. Kitty died in 1915, and Hershey never remarried. Shortly after her death, he donated his entire fortune to the school and expanded it to serve children of both sexes from kindergarten through high school.

The Hersheys were to travel on the ill-fated luxury liner the *Titanic* in 1912 but canceled because Mrs. Hershey became ill. The Hershey museum displays a copy of the check Hershey wrote as a deposit for a stateroom on the *Titanic*.

During the Great Depression, Hershey embarked on a building project that included a hotel, a high school, community building, a sports arena, and a new office building. The Hotel Hershey incorporated his favorite details from hotels worldwide. Mr. Hershey would later boast proudly that none of his workers were ever laid off during the Depression. On the contrary, he hired six hundred additional laborers.

Here is the grave of America's chocolate king who was lucky enough to miss his passage on the Titanic.

Hershey Chocolate supplied the U.S. Military with chocolate bars during World War II. They developed an unmeltable, four-ounce bar with extra calories and vitamins, which could be used as emergency provisions. Over three billion of the "Field Ration D" bars and "Tropical Bars" were produced and distributed to military personnel throughout the world. The U.S. Government gave Hershey the Army/Navy E award for his civilian contribution to the war effort.

Milton Hershey died in Hershey, Pennsylvania, on October 13, 1945, one year after his retirement as chairman of the board. He was 88 years old. He is buried in a beautiful grave in Hershey Cemetery.

In 1995, Milton Hershey was honored again by being pictured on a postage stamp commemorating him as a part of the U.S. Postal Service's Great Americans series.

In 2011, the Hershey Company topped six billion dollars in sales. That's a lot of chocolate!

If You Go:

Rival candy maker, Harry Reese, is buried near Milton Hershey in Hershey Cemetery. Reese founded H.B. Reese Candy Company around 1917. During the mid-twenties, he started to make an item called the Reese's Peanut Butter Cup. Reese died in 1956, and six years later, the company was sold to Hershey Chocolate for $235 million.

Hershey has an abundance of great places to eat and drink, and we have visited many of them—some numerous times. The majestic Hershey Hotel and grounds is itself a sight to see. We recommend the Iberian Lounge as a place to relax and unwind. Expertly prepared cocktails (yes, even a chocolate martini), plush seating, and a roaring fireplace make you feel special.

Devon Seafood Grill offers premium seafood and drinks in an upscale casual atmosphere and is in the same building (the Hershey Press Building on Chocolate Ave) as the always fun and reliable Houlihan's Restaurant and Bar.

A few blocks away on Cocoa Avenue is another fun place with a great menu, Fire Alley. It's a casual, fun atmosphere with booths and tables and even bench seating at the bars. We love it. We also love Overtime Sports Bar at 312 Mill St. Plenty of TVs, a great bar menu, and a friendly neighborhood atmosphere.

Also, about twenty minutes from Hershey in Mechanicsburg at 6108 Carlisle Pike is a great place called Black N Bleu. The theme is "Black Tie or Bleu Collar, come as you are." A great menu (had a hard time deciding) and a nice selection of beers and wines served by an attentive, friendly staff make this an experience we want to have again and again.

This is the memorial to children who passed away while attending the Milton Hershey School

12.

JOHNSTOWN FLOOD VICTIMS

"An Act of God?"

County: Cambria • Town: Johnstown
Buried at Grandview Cemetery
801 Millcreek Road

Heavy rainfall caused water to rise in the streets of Johnstown, Pennsylvania, in late May 1889. That seemed normal and didn't raise any alarms. Being built on the fork of Little Conemaugh and Stonycreek Rivers, flooding had been a problem since its founding. On June 1, 1889, Americans woke to the news that Johnstown had been devastated by the worst flood in the nation's history. A neglected dam and phenomenal storm led to a catastrophe in which 2,209 people died. It's a story of great tragedy, and when the full story came to light, many believed that if it was a "natural" disaster, then surely man was an accomplice.

The Little Conemaugh and the Stonycreek Rivers meet in Johnstown and form the Conemaugh River. In 1889, Johnstown was a town of Welsh and German immigrants with a population of about 30,000, including surrounding towns. High above the city, the South Fork Dam was built by the Commonwealth of Pennsylvania between 1838 and 1853 as part of a cross-state canal system. The reservoir behind the dam, Lake Conemaugh, supplied water to the city.

As railroads replaced canal barge transportation, the canal was abandoned by the Commonwealth and sold to the Pennsylvania Railroad. The dam and the lake were subsequently sold to private interests. One of the private interests was a group led by Henry Clay Frick, chairman of Carnegie Brothers Company, who had made a fortune selling coke. They intended to modify the lake and convert it into a private resort for the wealthy of Pittsburgh. They formed the South Fork Fishing and Hunting Club and bought it in 1879. The purpose of the club was to provide the members and their families an opportunity to escape the noise, heat, and dirt of Pittsburgh. There were sixty-one members at that time, including Andrew Carnegie, Henry Clay Frick, Andrew Mellon, Philander Chase Knox (who served as U.S. Attorney General, U.S. Senator, and Secretary of State), and Benjamin Thaw, the uncle of Harry Thaw (see Chapter 24). They built a 47-room clubhouse with a huge dining room and 16 houses along the lake's shores. The club's boat fleet included a pair of steam yachts, many sailboats, and canoes and the boathouses to house them. The club did engage in some periodic maintenance of the dam, but also made some harmful modifications to it. They lowered the dam to make its top wide enough to hold a road, and they installed fish screens across the spillway to keep expensive game fish from escaping, which had the unfortunate effect of capturing debris keeping the spillway from draining the lake's overflow.

On May 30th, 1889, unusually heavy rains hit the area. The U.S. Army Signal Corps estimated six to ten inches of rain fell in 24 hours. At

Detail of The Great Conemaugh Valley Disaster—Flood & Fire at Johnstown, Pa., subtitled Hundreds Roasted Alive at the Railroad Bridge. Reproduced from a lithograph print published by Kurz & Allison Art Publishers, 76 & 78 Wabash Avenue, Chicago, Illinois.

around 3:10 P.M., the South Fork Dam burst. The collapse sent twenty million tons of water roaring downstream toward Johnstown. On its way, it picked up debris, such as trees, rocks, houses, and animals. When it hit Johnstown, it was about forty feet high and a half-mile wide and traveling about 40 miles an hour. Just outside of East Conemaugh, a locomotive engineer, John Hess, was sitting in his locomotive. He heard the rumbling of the approaching flood and, correctly assuming what it was, tried to warn people by blowing the train whistle and racing toward the town riding backward. His warning saved many people who were able to get to high ground. Hess himself miraculously survived despite the locomotive being picked up and tossed aside by the wall of water and debris. At 4:07 P.M., the wall of water hit Johnstown. At first, it sounded like a low rumble that grew to a roar like thunder.

It was over in ten minutes, but for some, the worst was still yet to come. Darkness fell, thousands were huddled in attics, others floating on the debris, while many more had been swept downstream to the old stone bridge at the junction of the rivers. There, much of the debris piled up against the arches and caught fire, killing eighty people who had survived the initial flood wave. The fire burned for three days. The pile of debris reached seventy feet in height and took three months to remove because of the masses of steel wire from an ironworks factory binding it. Dynamite was eventually used to clear it.

Many bodies were never identified, hundreds of the missing never found. The official death toll registered 2,209 people killed or presumed lost. Among the dead were 99 entire families, 396 children under the age of ten, and 777 unidentified victims.

Emergency morgues and hospitals were set up, and commissaries distributed food and clothing. Across the country and around the world, people responded with a spontaneous outpouring of time, money, food, clothing, and medical assistance. A total of $3.7 million was collected from the U.S. and eighteen foreign countries.

The American Red Cross, which was formed in 1881 by Clara Barton, arrived in Johnstown on June 5, five days after the disaster. This was the group's first major disaster relief effort, and Clara Barton herself

Debris being removed from the railroad bridge.

was to lead the relief efforts. She and many other volunteers worked tirelessly and didn't leave for more than five months.

The media response to the disaster was immediate. Over 100 newspapers and magazines sent writers and illustrators to Johnstown. The Johnstown Flood was the biggest news story since the Civil War. The dead were lined up in morgues throughout the city and in communities further down the river until some survivor in search of a loved one came to identify them. The living set up tents, often near the place their homes had been located and began the task of cleaning up and starting life again. Although not noted for their accuracy, the reports touched the hearts of readers. Residents of Johnstown and Americans, in general, began to turn their wrath on the members of the South Fork Fishing and Hunting Club. Newspapers across the country denounced the sportsmen's lake. The *Chicago Herald's* editorial on the disaster was entitled "Manslaughter or Murder?" On June 9, the *Herald* carried a cartoon that showed the members of the club drinking champagne on the porch of the clubhouse while, in the valley beneath them, the flood is destroying Johnstown. A *New York World* headline on June 7 declared, "The Club is Guilty."

Debris on Main Street.

In the immediate aftermath of the tragedy, the club contributed 1,000 blankets to the relief effort. A few of the club members served on relief committees. Only about half the club members contributed to the disaster relief effort, including Andrew Carnegie, whose company gave $10,000 and who later rebuilt Johnstown's library. However, no club member ever expressed a sense of personal responsibility for the disaster.

The club had very few assets aside from the clubhouse, but a few lawsuits were brought against the club anyway. Legal action against individual club members was difficult as it would have been necessary to prove personal negligence—and the power and influence of the club members are hard to overestimate. Despite the accusations and the evidence, they were successfully defended by the firm of Knox and Reed, both partners of which were club members (Philander Knox and James Reed). The Club was never held legally responsible for the disaster. The court held the dam break to have been an act of God and granted the survivors no legal compensation.

Many bodies were never identified, and hundreds of the missing never found. The cleanup operation took years with bodies being found months later and, in a few cases, years after the flood. In 1989, on the 100th anniversary of the flood, 106-year-old survivor Elsie Frum was interviewed by news organizations. Her father was alerted by John Hess's train whistle and had gotten his family to safety, thus saving young Elsie's life. Frank Shomo, reportedly the last survivor of the Johnstown Flood, died in 1997 at the age of 108.

There is a large, beautiful memorial marking the resting place of 777 flood victims who could not be identified in Grandview Cemetery in Johnstown. The State Flood Commission purchased the plot,

Memorial to 777 unidentified victims of the Johnstown flood.

called "The Unknown Plot," for burying the unidentified and bought markers for each grave. It was dedicated on May 31, 1892, exactly three years after the flood.

The Johnstown Flood Museum is located on Washington Street in Johnstown in a large beautiful brick building that was built for the city, as the new library, by Andrew Carnegie. The museum provides exhibits and artifacts that tell the story of the flood, and the film *The Johnstown Flood*, winner of the 1989 Academy Award for Best Documentary Short Subject, is shown each hour at the museum's theater. The Johnstown Flood National Memorial is located about ten miles northeast of Johnstown. The park preserves the remains of the South Fork Dam. The visitor center features multi-media exhibits, including a fiber-optic map, which describes the path of the flood.

If You Go:

Grandview Cemetery is the final resting place of Congressional Medal of Honor recipient George W. Reed. Reed was awarded his medal for his bravery in action at the Second Battle of Weldon Railroad, Virginia, during the siege of Petersburg in the Civil War in 1864.

There is also an impressive grave marking the remains of Boyd "Buzz" Wagner, the World War II fighter ace. Wagner rose to lieutenant colonel in the Army Air Corps during World War II. He shot down eight Japanese planes and earned the title as America's first fighter ace. He was a recipient of the Purple Heart and the Distinguished Flying Cross. John McCrory, the founder of the McCrory Five and Ten Cent store chain, is also buried there in the family mausoleum above whose entrance is inscribed "McCrorey," the original spelling of the family name. His hundreds of stores would come to be known as the second of the great five-and-dime chain stores following Woolworths and preceding Kresge.

Pete Duranko, the Notre Dame All-American from the 1966 national championship team and eight-year NFL veteran, is also buried in Grandview Cemetery, as is Congressman John Murtha. Murtha represented Pennsylvania in Congress for 36 years and was the first Vietnam Veteran elected to the U.S. House of Representatives.

Memorial to those who had their graves destroyed by the Johnstown flood.

13.

PHILIP LIVINGSTON
"A Little-Known Founding Father"

County: York • Town: York
Buried at Prospect Hill Cemetery
700 North George Street

Philip Livingston opposed violence and once said that independence was "a vain shallow and ridiculous project" and warned that America would collapse if separated from England.

On his first trip out of Massachusetts, John Adams was on his way to Philadelphia to serve as a member of the Continental Congress. On a stop in New York, he was able to arrange meetings with some of New York's representatives that would serve in Congress with him. Among these was Philip Livingston. Adams found that Livingston not only opposed revolution but that he distrusted New Englanders. Livingston questioned Adams as to why Massachusetts had once hanged Quakers and used the incident to argue that a revolution would only result in the colonies fighting each other. Adams later said that it was impossible to reason with Livingston. However, the behavior of the British government eventually turned the New Yorker into an ardent patriot and an active promoter of efforts to raise and fund troops for the war.

Livingston was born on January 15, 1716, in Albany, New York, into a prosperous family. His father, Robert Livingston, had emigrated to America from Scotland in 1673. He settled in Albany and quickly established himself in the fur trade. In 1687 the English Royal Governor granted him ownership of a tract of land consisting of 160,000 acres on the east bank of the Hudson River. The land became known as the Manor of Livingston and remains in the family to the present day.

Philip Livingston

Robert saw to it that young Philip was tutored at home and then attended and graduated from Yale University in 1737. After marrying Christina Broeck, the daughter of the mayor of Albany, the couple settled in New York City, where he became a very successful merchant and took an active part in civic affairs. His accomplishments during this time included pushing for the founding of Kings College (known today as Columbia University), the establishment of a Professorship of Divinity at Yale, the building of the first meeting house for the Methodist Society in America, and providing aid to organize the New York Public Library.

In 1754 he was elected an alderman in the city, his first venture into public life. He would continue to be elected alderman for nine consecutive years. His success in these elections suggests that he was perceived as an effective representative by those who were able to cast ballots. In 1758 he was also elected to the colonial legislature and would urge moderation in dealings with England.

In 1765 he attended the Stamp Act Congress, which produced the first formal protest to the crown. He was elected to the First and Second Continental Congress, and during this time, he changed his mind and supported the Revolution and signed the Declaration of Independence in 1776.

Philip Livingston

Livingston spent a large part of his own money to purchase supplies for the army. When the British army captured New York, they seized his two houses, forcing his family to flee to Kingston. They used his Duke Street home as a barracks and his Brooklyn Heights residence as a Royal Navy Hospital.

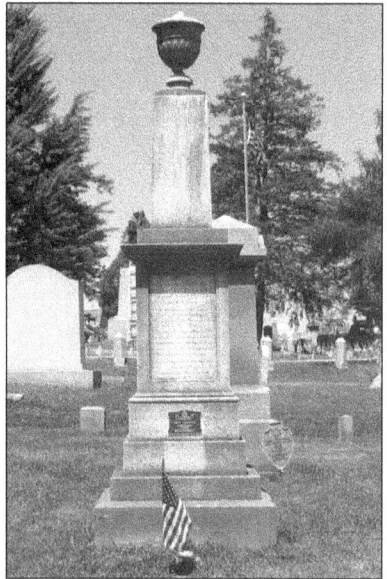

Here is the grave of Philip Livingston, a man who represented New York in the Continental Congress.

Unfortunately, Livingston did not live to see the American victory. He was elected to Congress in October 1777. During this particularly critical and gloomy period in the Revolution, Congress was forced to meet in York, Pennsylvania, because the British had seized Philadelphia. Livingston's health was precarious, as he was diagnosed with dropsy in the chest (today it would be called congestive heart failure) with no rational prospect of recovery or improvement. Yet his love of his country was unwavering, and so he did not hesitate to give up the comforts of home and family.

With his health declining, he made the trip to York after bidding his friends and family a final farewell. He believed he would never return. He proved to be correct; on June 12, 1778, Philip Livingston died. He was sixty-two years old. The entire Congress attended his funeral and declared a mourning period of a month. He was first buried in a churchyard at the German Reformed Church on West Market Street in York but later moved to Prospect Hill Cemetery in York. In 2005, Descendants of the Signers of the Declaration of Independence honored him by attaching a plaque to his tombstone, identifying him as a Signer of the Declaration. A few of the direct descendants took part in the dedication ceremony.

If You Go:
Prospect Hill Cemetery was a pleasant surprise. It is a well-maintained, operating cemetery where Greg Miller and Steliana Vassileva were extremely helpful. We knew there were Civil War Congressional Medal of Honor recipients buried there, and they helped us find their graves. John Henry Denig was awarded the Congressional Medal of Honor for his actions in Mobile Bay on August 5, 1864, while serving on the USS *Brooklyn*. Charles Henry Ilgenfritz was awarded the Congressional Medal of Honor for action at Fort Sedgwick, Virginia, on April 2, 1865. He was a sergeant in Company E, 207th, Pennsylvania Infantry.

While searching for these graves, we discovered that inside Prospect Hill was Soldiers Circle—a federally-owned site given to America after the Civil War as a final resting place for soldiers who died of their wounds after the Battle of Gettysburg. There are more than 162 Union soldiers buried there. The monument, which consists of a fifteen-foot bronze figure of a soldier surrounded by four cannons, was erected in 1874 to honor the Union troops, most of whom died in the hospital established in York in 1862 to care for the Civil War wounded. This is

*This is Soldiers Circle which is a National Cemetery
located in Prospect Hill Cemetery in York.*

now a National Civil War Landmark. While we were there, it was being restored by the U.S. Department of Veteran's Affairs.

There are also five unknown Confederate casualties from Gettysburg buried in a mass grave in another part of Prospect Hill cemetery. York was the site of an army hospital during the Civil War. Wounded soldiers from the Battle of Gettysburg were dispersed among various hospitals in the north as soon as the patients were healthy enough for the journey. However, the director of the hospital, army surgeon Dr. Henry Palmer of the famed Iron Brigade, refused to allow any wounded rebels to be taken to his facility and threatened to resign if forced to accept them. Five of them died. It seems that Dr. Palmer had been taken prisoner by Jubal Early's rebels on June 28 when the Confederates moved into York. He escaped during the Gettysburg battle and returned to his job in York. You might say he bore a grudge.

Also buried at Prospect Hill is Navy Seal Petty Officer 1st Class Neil C. Roberts who was shot and killed in 2002 by al-Qaida forces in the Khawar Mountains of Afghanistan in the Battle of Takur Ghar which

*This tombstone in Prospect Hill Cemetery in York marks
the final resting place of five unknown confederate soldiers.*

is also known as The Battle of Roberts Ridge. He was posthumously awarded the Bronze Star.

Friends had told us if we were ever in York and thirsty or hungry to try The Left Bank Restaurant on North George St. We did, and our friends proved to be very wise. The food, drinks, décor, and service were all top rate.

Saints be praised if just down the street we didn't see an Irish pub called Maewyn's and thought it a sin if we didn't stop in and have a pint. The beer and the hospitality were wonderful, and the wait staff wore kilts. It made us just a wee bit proud.

14.

MICHAEL MAGGIO
ANTONIO POLLINA
ANGELO BRUNO
PHILIP TESTA
SALVATORE TESTA

"Philadelphia's Sinners"

County: Delaware • Town: Yeadon
Buried at Holy Cross Cemetery
626 Bailey Road

"Well, they blew up the chicken man in Philly last night; now they blew up his house too." These are the lyrics that open the classic Bruce Springsteen song "Atlantic City." The song was released in 1982, a year after the violent death of Philip "Chicken Man" Testa. Testa was killed in his home by a bomb. He and at least four other reputed Philadelphia Mafia figures are buried in Holy Cross Cemetery in Yeadon.

Michael Maggio was reputedly an old-time mafia don from the 1920s until 1959. In 1934, Maggio, who was known as the "Cheese King" because of his successful cheese business, was arrested for the murder of his second wife, Anna, 32, and son, Joseph, 21, from a prior marriage. As the story goes, Maggio suspected them of having an affair, and after catching them in bed, he shot and killed them both. He pleaded guilty, and was sentenced to five years, but served less than two.

Maggio is credited with sponsoring a future mob boss, Angelo Bruno, for membership in the organization. At that time, the active boss of the Philadelphia mafia family was Salvatore Sabella. Bruno was a salesman for Maggio's cheese company and put in a good word to Sabella regarding

Ruins at the Testa house.

Bruno's hard work ethic. Shortly after that, Bruno was running several small operations for Sabella. Michael Maggio died of natural causes at the age of 69 in 1959. He is buried in a large beautiful mausoleum with a large stained-glass window.

Antonio Pollina accomplished what most people would never expect of the head of a crime family; he lived to be 100 years old. Known as "Mr. Migs," Pollina was named don by Guiseppe "Joe Ida" Idda shortly before Idda fled to Italy to avoid being indicted by federal authorities. Despite being named the boss, Pollina considered Angelo Bruno a rival, and ordered his underboss to kill him. The underboss, Ignazio Denaro, informed Bruno and Bruno told "the Commission," a national mafia board formed to resolve disputes among organized crime families and members. The Commission decided to remove Pollina and make Bruno the new boss of Philadelphia and advised him he could have Pollina killed for plotting against him. Bruno decided to let Pollina live, figuring the repercussion would be bad for the family. Pollina remained inactive in the mob for the rest of his life. He was a suspect in several murders over the years but was never convicted. He died in 1993 at the age of 100.

Angelo Bruno was born Angelo Annaloro in Sicily and emigrated to the United States in his early teens, settling in Philadelphia. After being named the new boss of the Philadelphia family in 1959, he assumed the

surname of his paternal grand-
mother and became Angelo
Bruno.

Over the next twenty years,
Bruno avoided the intense
media and law enforcement
scrutiny and outbursts that
plagued other crime families.
He was known for instituting
order and increasing the power
of the Philadelphia mob family and connections to larger,
more established families in
New York and New Jersey. He
was given the nickname "The
Gentle Don" as he preferred
to settle disputes in a professional, non-violent manner.
He also avoided lengthy
prison terms despite several
arrests. His longest term was
two years for refusing to testify
to a grand jury. Under Bruno,
the Philadelphia crime family enjoyed the most peaceful
and prosperous reign. Bruno

This man was known as the Cheese King. He killed his wife and son (by a previous marriage) for sleeping with each other.

Known as Mister Migs, this crime family head lived to the ripe old age of 100.

did not allow his family to deal narcotics, preferring more traditional
operations like labor racketeering, illegal gambling, extortion, bookmak-
ing, and loansharking. His philosophy was to "make money; don't make
headlines." His position on narcotics, however, eroded some of his support since many factions below him felt they should have a piece of the
action. Then, in 1976, Atlantic City, New Jersey, opened for gambling,
and soon it became so lucrative that he agreed to let the New York and
New Jersey families share in the profits. Bruno knew better than to try to

challenge the New York families who were a lot stronger than his. This decision did not go over well with many of his underlings and further eroded his support. Several factions within the Pennsylvania family began conspiring to betray the aging Bruno.

On March 21, 1980, the 69-year-old Bruno was killed by a shotgun blast in the back of the head as he sat in his car in front of his south Philadelphia home. It is believed that the killing was ordered by Antonio Caponigro (aka Tony Bananas), Bruno's consigliere. A few weeks later, Caponigro's body was found stuffed in a body bag in the trunk of a car in New York City with about $300 jammed into his mouth and anus. The Commission reportedly ordered his murder because he assassinated Bruno without full permission. Other Philadelphia family members involved in Bruno's murder were tortured and killed.

Angelo Bruno (right)

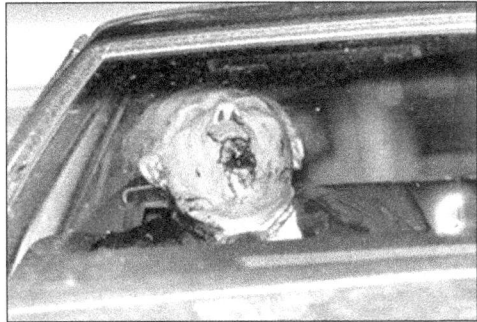

Crime scene photo of Angelo Bruno.

Known as the Gentle Don, Bruno was killed by a shotgun blast to the back of the head. It appears that he had friends who were not so gentle.

Philip "The Chicken Man" Testa took over as mob boss in Philadelphia after the death of Angelo Bruno. He was born in Sicily and emigrated to the U.S. and settled in south Philadelphia in his teenage years. He was a dour-looking man with a pockmarked face. He stood about five feet, eight inches, and weighed 183 pounds. He reportedly had dark emotionless eyes and a pockmarked face, which is thought to be one of the reasons for his nickname. The pockmarks are believed to have been caused by a horrible case of chickenpox with the scars never fully healing. He had a thick mustache and preferred blue-collar clothing to the fancy clothing worn by most mafia dons. He became a father to his only son, Salvatore, in 1956, and they were very close. He was a staunch Roman Catholic and raised his son in the same fashion. He reportedly did not drink heavily and remained loyal to

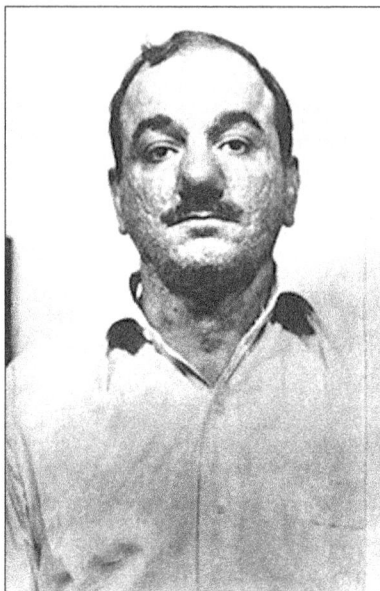

Philip "Chicken Man" Testa

his wife. Testa conducted his business, legitimate and otherwise, out of a restaurant, which he owned and his daughter Maria managed, in Old City Philadelphia.

In February 1981, Testa was indicted by Federal authorities for racketeering. The case was based on an investigation called Operation Gangplank and was one of the first built on the RICO Act by the U.S. Attorney's office in Philadelphia. On March 15, 1981, less than a year after the murder of Angelo Bruno, Philip Testa was killed by a bomb exploding in his home across the street from Stephen Girard Park. There were roofing nails in the bomb that were to make it look like retaliation by allies of John McCullough, the roofing union leader who was killed mob-style in December 1980. Testa's killing touched off a string of intra-family wars that lasted until 1995.

Salvatore "Salvie" Testa became a rising star in the mob after his father's murder. A 1974 graduate of Saint John Neumann High School, Salvie was a ruggedly handsome man who was six feet tall and 210 pounds. His parents had chosen Nicky Scarfo and his wife Domenica as his godparents. After the murder of his father, Salvie became a protégé of Nick Scarfo and was thought of like a son to Scarfo. Scarfo made him a captain (caporegime) a few months after his father's death. Newspaper accounts say that Scarfo used Salvie for over fifteen hits. He had "inherited" most of his father's business and an estate worth $800,000 that included a rundown bar in Atlantic City on a site where casino developer Donald Trump decided to build the Trump Plaza in 1984. Trump paid the young Testa $1.1 million for the right to tear it down.

Salvatore Testa with a couple escorts.

Two of the hits were the men responsible for killing his father. On January 7, 1982, Chickie Narducci, the man who reportedly orchestrated the killing of Philip Testa, was shot ten times in the face, neck, and chest outside his home in south Philadelphia. On March

Here lies "Chicken Man" Testa and his son Salvie. Notice the grave goods left on the tomb.

15, 1982, exactly one year after the bombing, Rocco Marinucci, the man who reportedly detonated the bomb, was found dead in a parking lot on Federal Street in Philadelphia. He had bullet wounds to the neck, chest, and head, and his mouth was stuffed with three large, unexploded cherry bombs.

In April 1984, Salvie Testa was described as the "fastest rising star" in the Philadelphia mob in a front-page article of the *Wall Street Journal*. This made Nicky Scarfo jealous and worried that Testa was becoming too powerful, especially with his group of young Turks. According to newspaper accounts, on September 14, 1984, Scarfo ordered Testa's best friend, Joey Pungitore, to lure Testa into an ambush in the back room of the Too Sweet candy store on East Passyunk Avenue in Philadelphia. Scarfo had requested that his godson be strangled to death, but his killers considered this too risky given Salvie's size and strength. His hog-tied body was found at the side of a dirt road in Gloucester Township, New Jersey. He was wrapped in a carpet with a rope around his neck. He had been shot twice in the back of the head. He was 28 years old.

In May of 1988, Scarfo and eight associates were acquitted on all charges in the murder of Testa. A book about the Philadelphia mob was published in 2003. It's titled *Blood and Honor: Inside the Scarfo Mob— The Mafia's Most Violet Family* by George Anastasia.

If You Go:

Holy Cross Cemetery is a large and well-maintained cemetery with many interesting graves (see Chapter 16 for the story of Dr. Henry Holmes). One such grave is that of Louis Van Zelst, who was the batboy and mascot for the Philadelphia Athletics from 1910 to 1914. Due to a childhood accident, his growth was stunted, and he had a hunchback. He loved sports and wandered over to Shibe Park one day in 1909 and asked Connie Mack if he could be a batboy. Mack took an instant liking to Van Zelst and agreed. In the early part of the century, hunchbacks were good luck, and

Here lies the Philadelphia Athletics first mascot, players used to rub his hunchback for good luck.

players would rub the hump for luck. He became a favorite of the A's players and fans, and the next year, 1910, Mack hired him for all home games and had a uniform made for him. As luck would have it, the A's won their first world championship that year, repeated in 1911 and 1913, and won the American League pennant in 1914. He was taken on at least one road trip per year from early 1911 and to spring training in 1912. He had a sunny disposition and was an accomplished mimic who did a hysterical imitation of Eddie Plank in the batter's box. In the five years he was with the A's, they won four pennants and three World Series. In the winter of 1915, he was diagnosed with Bright's disease and died in March. Connie Mack and the team were crestfallen, and the A's next pennant didn't come until 1929.

There are four Congressional Medal of Honor recipients buried at Holy Cross. William Shipman, George Crawford Platt, and William Densmore all received their Medals of Honor for bravery in the Civil War. Philip Gaughan received his Medal of Honor for his courageous action in the Spanish-American War.

Frank Hardart of the famous Horn and Hardart restaurants is also buried in Holy Cross. In 1902, they opened the first American automat in Philadelphia. Hot entrees, cold sandwiches, bowls of soup, and slices of pie awaited behind the small glass doors, which opened when the right number of nickels were inserted. He died in 1918.

Also, there are two Hall of Fame Boxers and the youngest U.S. Open Golf Champion of all time. The boxers are light Heavyweight Champion Thomas Loughran, who is regarded as one of the most skilled fighters of all time and died in 1982, and Joseph "Philadelphia Jack" Hagen, who was also the World Light Heavyweight Champion from 1905–1912. Hagen died in 1942. The golfer John McDermott was the first U.S.-born golfer to win the U.S. Open and the youngest ever, at 19 years ten months, in 1911. His story will be a full chapter in a future volume of Keystone Tombstones.

15.

ROBERT MORRIS
AND
JAMES WILSON

"Founding Fathers"

County: Philadelphia • Town: Philadelphia
Both buried at Christ Episcopal Church and Churchyard
20 North American Street (On 2nd, above Market Street)

Both men were born in Europe. They both came to America because of the opportunities the New World had to offer. They both settled in Philadelphia. They were both successful: one as a businessman, the other as an attorney. Both men were also successful in the field of Pennsylvania politics. Both men signed the Declaration of Independence and the United States Constitution. Their names are Robert Morris and James Wilson, and they were truly Founding Fathers.

Robert Morris was born in Liverpool, England, on January 20, 1734. When he was thirteen years of age, he joined his father in Maryland. His father sent him to Philadelphia to stay with a family friend named Charles Greenway. Morris then became an apprentice for the Philadelphia merchant and Philadelphia mayor Charles Willing. Charles Willing died in 1854, and his son Thomas Willing made Morris a partner in the firm. On May 1, 1757, the two businessmen established the shipping and banking firm of Willing, Morris, & Company. The two would remain partners until 1779.

The new company's shipping business was involved in the slave trade. The company funded a slave-trading voyage, but the trip turned out to be unprofitable. On a second voyage, their ship was captured by French

James Wilson

Robert Morris

pirates. The company did handle several slave auctions for other import-ers. In 1765 they were involved in their last deal involving slaves when they advertised seventy slaves for sale. Records indicate the slaves were not sold in Philadelphia but sent to Jamaica. Both Willing and Morris supported non-importation agreements, which resulted in the end of all trade with England, including the importation of slaves.

In 1769 at the age of 35, Morris married the 20-year-old Mary White. They would have seven children together: five sons and two daughters. White came from a well-respected family in Maryland; her brother was a well-known bishop named William White. Morris worshipped at Saint Peter's Church in Philadelphia, which was run by his brother-in-law. Both Morris and William White were later buried in the churchyard. When the Continental Congress was in session, many of its members worshiped there, including George Washington.

Morris first became involved in politics when England passed the Stamp Act of 1765–1776. It imposed a tax on all legal documents. Morris served on a committee of merchants established to oppose the tax. In one instance, he served as a mediator between a mass of protesters and the stamp tax collector. The protesters were threatening to tear down the home of the collector. Morris was able to resolve the dispute peacefully by getting the collector to agree not to collect the tax. Morris was still a loyal British subject, but he believed this tax constituted taxation without representation, and, in a short time, the tax was repealed.

Morris was warden of the port of Philadelphia. When the tea tax was passed, and a ship carrying tea entered the Delaware Bay, orders were issued that the ship should not be brought to port. The captain of the ship followed another ship up the channel, which set up a large public protest in Philadelphia. The captain was taken to the State House, where he met with a group that included Morris. After the meeting, the captain agreed to leave the city and to take his tea with him.

Morris now became very active in Pennsylvania politics. He served in the Pennsylvania legislature from 1776 to 1778. He was also elected as a Pennsylvania representative to the Second Continental Congress, where he served from 1775 to 1778. While in Congress, he devised a system to enable the Americans to smuggle war supplies provided by France. He also sold his best ship, *The Black Prince*, to the Congress, and it became the first ship in the Continental Navy.

On July 1, 1776, Morris voted against the motion for independence, which resulted in Pennsylvania voting against the measure. The following day when a similar vote was taken, John Dickinson and Morris abstained, which put Pennsylvania in favor of independence as the motion passed unanimously. When Morris signed the Declaration of Independence, he said, "I am not one of those politicians that run testy when my own plans are not adopted. I think it is the duty of a good citizen to follow when he cannot lead."

During the fight for independence, Morris became known as the "Financier of the Revolution." From 1781 to 1784, he was the Superintendent of Finance, and it was his responsibility to manage the young country's economy. During the Revolution, he loaned the country $10,000 to pay the troops Washington had assembled. He also donated personal funds for the same purpose. Morris saw his wealth increase during these times as a result of privateers who attacked and seized the cargo of British ships during the Revolution. Morris owned at least an interest in many of the ships used by privateers, and he also was involved in selling the goods seized from the British. Thomas Paine and others would later accuse Morris of war profiteering, but a congressional committee acquitted Morris of these charges in 1779.

Morris played an important part in getting Washington's army from New York to Yorktown, Virginia. He was with Washington the day the army went on the move, and he acted as quartermaster. He also used $1,400,000 of his credit to move the army. This would not be the last time that he used personal funds to aid in the war effort, and the use of his fortune strained his finances.

While Morris was Superintendent of Finance, he was assisted by a friend named Gouverneur Morris (they were not related). Together they proposed the creation of a national economic system. This proposal served as the basis for the system started by Alexander Hamilton when he became Secretary of the Treasury. Morris also pushed for the establishment of a national mint, a recommendation that was finally adopted in 1792 after being pushed by Hamilton and Thomas Jefferson.

In 1787 Morris was elected as a Pennsylvanian representative to the Constitutional Convention. He was also instrumental in getting Gouverneur Morris selected as a member of Pennsylvania's delegation. Robert Morris nominated his friend George Washington to be president of the convention. When the Constitution was adopted, both Morris and Gouverneur Morris were among the signers.

Washington wanted Morris to be his Secretary of the Treasury in 1789, but Morris turned down the offer and suggested the appointment of Alexander Hamilton, a man who supported most of Morris's policies. Morris served as a United States Senator, representing Pennsylvania from 1789 to 1795. He supported the economic program set forth by the Federalist party that resulted in internal improvements such as canals to improve commerce.

Morris became heavily involved in unsuccessful land speculations. He invested heavily in the western territories and soon found that he was unable to sell the lands or afford to pay the taxes on them. Morris's rise in America had been spectacular, and so was his fall. Hounded by creditors, he was arrested and placed in a debtor's prison in Philadelphia from February 1798 to August 1801. In 1800 the United States Congress passed a temporary Bankruptcy Act which, once enacted, resulted in his release from prison. Morris was in poor health and spent his remaining years in retirement. He died on May 8, 1806, in Philadelphia and was laid to rest in the Christ Episcopal Churchyard.

Here is the grave of Robert Morris who helped fund the Continental Army during the American Revolution.

James Wilson was born on September 14, 1742, in Carskerdo, Scotland. He attended several Scottish universities, including Edinburgh and Saint Andrews, but never graduated with a degree. Wilson arrived in America in 1766 at the age of 21 and settled in Philadelphia. He found work teaching at The Academy and College of Philadelphia, which is now the University of Pennsylvania. The University awarded him an honorary Master of Arts degree.

Wilson decided to study law, and he did so at the office of John Dickinson. After gaining admittance to the bar, he set up a law practice in Reading, Pennsylvania, in 1767. His practice was very successful, and he bought a small farm near Carlisle, Pennsylvania. He was soon handling law cases in eight counties while he continued to lecture at The Academy and College of Philadelphia. In 1771 he married, and he and his wife had six children together.

Wilson was quick to take up the revolutionary cause. In 1768 he authored *Considerations on the Nature and Extent of the Legislative Authority of the British Parliament*. The work was published in 1774, and it concluded that Parliament had no authority to pass laws governing the colonies because the colonies were not represented in Parliament. Wilson put forth his view that all power is derived from the people. He also had a very different view of what the English Empire could be. In describing his vision, he wrote, "Distinct states independent of each other but connected under the same sovereign." Years later, at America's Constitutional Convention, he would raise this idea again.

Wilson was a member of the Continental Congress in 1776. In Congress, he was considered one of the "cool devils," a name attached to representatives who worked to delay independence. This group angered John Adams. During this time, Wilson caucused his district to determine where those he represented stood on the question of independence. After receiving this information, he voted for independence. During his time in Congress, he served on the Committee on Spies with Thomas Jefferson, John Rutledge, John Adams, and Robert Livingston. Their committee defined what was considered treason for the young country.

In 1779, after the British left Philadelphia, Wilson successfully defended 23 people from property seizure in an action that was initiated by the government of Pennsylvania. As a result, on October 4, 1779, a mob attacked Wilson's home. Wilson and 35 of his friends barricaded themselves in what would later be called Fort Wilson. During the fight that followed, six people were killed, and many more were wounded. The city's soldiers eventually drove the mob away. The rioters were pardoned by Joseph Reed, who was then the president of Pennsylvania's Supreme Executive Council.

Wilson was considered to possess one of the great legal minds of his time. Also, the study of government had become a passion for him. As a result, he was one of the most active delegates at the Constitutional Convention that began in May of 1787. Wilson addressed the convention 168 times on the numerous issues that the delegates had to address. He favored a single executive, and he wanted the president and senators to be elected through the popular vote. Doctor Benjamin Rush, who also attended the convention, described Wilson's mind as "one blaze of light." On the day of the vote to adopt the Constitution, Benjamin Franklin had composed a speech urging its passage. Franklin did not feel up to giving the speech himself, so he had Wilson read it on his behalf.

Wilson, like many of the delegates to the convention, was not fully satisfied with the Constitution. Despite his reservations, he worked hard to make sure that Pennsylvania would accept the document. His efforts met with success when Pennsylvania became the second state to ratify the Constitution. Despite the ratification, many Pennsylvanians remained opposed to the new form of government. On December 27, 1787, an outdoor rally was held in Carlisle to celebrate the Constitution. A group of men armed with clubs attacked and began beating Wilson. Wilson later said he would have been killed if not for an old soldier who threw his body over Wilson's and absorbed many of the blows.

President Washington nominated Wilson to be a justice on the United States Supreme Court on September 24, 1789. He was confirmed by the United States Senate and served on the court until 1798. During that time, only nine cases were heard by the highest court in the land.

Much like Morris, Wilson's final days were filled with financial failures. He, too, found himself deep in debt as a result of land speculation.

This is the grave of James Wilson, signer of both the Declaration of Independence and the United State's Constitution.

Wilson fled to North Carolina to escape his creditors. It was in North Carolina while visiting a friend that Wilson suffered a stroke and died at the age of 55. He was originally buried in North Carolina, but in 1906 he was re-interred in the Christ Episcopal Churchyard in Philadelphia.

If You Go:
See chapters 7 and 14 titled "Philadelphia Saints" and "Philadelphia's Sinners." Also buried at Christ Episcopal Churchyard are two other signers of the United States Constitution, Pierce Butler, who was a representative from South Carolina, and Jacob Broom, who represented Delaware.

16.

HERMAN WEBSTER MUDGETT
(AKA DR. HENRY H. HOLMES)

"America's Answer to the Ripper"

County: Delaware • Town: Yeadon
Buried at Holy Cross Cemetery
626 Baily Road

One can reasonably argue that the most famous serial killer in history is Jack the Ripper. There have been numerous books written and films made about the Ripper. The actual Ripper was never found, and to this day, there are numerous theories as to who he was, and the suspects include members of the Royal Family. The Ripper murders began in the Whitechapel district of London in 1888, and some believe they continued until 1891. However, most who have studied the case believe the Ripper was responsible for only five of the ten murders in that time frame and that his last victim was killed on November 9, 1888.

In contrast, America's answer to the Ripper may have tortured and killed as many as 200 people, mostly young women. He was born Herman Webster Mudgett on May 16, 1861, in New Hampshire. However, during his killing spree, he went by the name Doctor Henry H. Holmes, and that is how we shall refer to him in this chapter.

Holmes was known as a bright boy with strange tendencies. His father was a violent alcoholic, and his mother a Methodist who would read the bible to the young boy. Holmes was bullied at school, and he went through several traumatic experiences as a child. He and one of his few close friends explored a deserted house one day, and Holmes watched his friend fall to his death from a landing in the home. Also, bullies dragged him into a doctor's office and forced him into the arms of a medical

Dr. Henry H. Holmes

skeleton. The bullies' goal was to scare him. Instead, he became obsessed with death.

As he hit his teens, his fascination with death manifested itself in the killing and dissection of animals. Holmes claimed his purpose in these mutilations was medical examination. Academically he continued to do well, and in 1884 he graduated with a medical degree from the University of Michigan in Ann Arbor. While at the university, he began an unusual business pursuit that would provide funds for him throughout his life. He began taking life insurance policies out on corpses in the medical school. He would steal the corpses and mutilate them in a manner to show they had died in an accident. Then he would make his claim to the insurance company.

Holmes married his first wife in 1878. She bore him a son named Robert Lovering Mudgett, who would go on to serve as city manager in Orlando, Florida. Holmes would marry two more times during his life without ever getting divorced. Also, he used his charm to prey on countless young women who fell for him and later died at his hands.

In 1886 Holmes moved to Chicago, where he found work as a drugstore assistant. E. S. Holton, the owner of the store, was dying of cancer, and his wife spent most of her time caring for her ailing husband. Holmes saw his opportunity, and he took it. When Holton died, Holmes persuaded Mrs. Horton to sell him the store. When the deal was complete, he murdered her and told those who asked about her that she had moved to California. In 1888 Holmes traveled to London, where he sold skeletons to medical schools. He returned to the states in December of that same year, a time frame that becomes important later in his story.

Now that he owned a drug store that was making a good profit, Holmes began putting his plan into place. He purchased a vacant lot across the street from his store, where he intended to build his "Castle." It was a three-story hotel that Holmes personally designed. The ground floor featured Holmes's drugstore. The second and third floors made up the hotel and featured secret passages, concealed chambers, staircases that led to brick walls, and soundproofed rooms with peepholes in the doors. Also, several of the rooms had been fitted with gas pipes that would allow Holmes to inject lethal gases into the area now of his choosing. The basement was an addition to this house of horrors. It contained a dissection chamber and pits of lime and acid as well as cremation furnaces. Holmes constructed the "Castle" by using multiple contractors. Once part of the building was complete, he would either fire or refuse payment to a contractor and hire another. As a result, no one could piece together

The infamous Murder Castle: Holmes Motel at 63rd & Wallace on Chicago's south side.

what Holmes planned to do in what would become known later as "the killing house."

The building was completed in time to take advantage of the many visitors to the 1893 Chicago World's Fair. The fair itself was a tremendous success and attracted visitors from all over the country. The fair marked the appearance of the first Ferris wheel, which was a gigantic machine compared to what we have today. For example, each of the 36 cars on the wheel could hold as many as sixty people. The cars were 24 feet long and 13 feet wide and weighed 26,000 pounds. The fair itself, whose buildings reflected the big dreams of the era, was known as the "White City" and even received praise from that great critic of the Gilded Age, Mark Twain. The owner of the new hotel, which he called the World's Fair Hotel, was eager to offer to house, and in many cases more, to those who chose to visit the fair.

Holmes didn't wait for the fair to open to begin more killings. In 1890 a man named Ned Connor went to work for Holmes as a watchmaker and jeweler. He and his very attractive wife named Julia and their daughter, Pearl, moved into an apartment above the drugstore. Holmes gave Julia a job as a bookkeeper and then seduced her. Ned Connor found out about the affair and left his wife and daughter. By this time in 1891, Holmes was living in the "Castle." He took out life insurance policies on Julia and Pearl that named him as the beneficiary. Around this time, Holmes began a relationship with a woman named Minnie Williams. Julia became angered by this turn of events, especially since she was carrying Holmes's child. Holmes convinced Julia to have an abortion that he would perform. He led her to the basement, where he aborted the child and killed Julia. He then killed Pearl using chloroform.

With his hotel now open, Holmes put his killing machine to work. Not only hotel staff but guests turned up missing. Holmes particularly enjoyed killing young women who he found attractive. Hotel staff were required to take out life insurance policies naming Holmes as the beneficiary. Holmes murdered his victims in a few ways. He gassed some in their rooms, he tortured some on a stretching rack he kept in the basement, he dissected a few victims while they were still alive and he also had some fireproof rooms so he could fill the room with gases, ignite the vapors, and burn the victim to death. The bodies were disposed of in his vats of acid or crematoriums. With some of his victims, he would remove the flesh and sell the skeletons to medical institutions. It is impossible to tell how many people he killed, but estimates range from 50 to 200.

When the World's Fair ended, the depression of 1893 was in full swing. With business way down at the hotel and his creditors on his back, Holmes left Chicago. He headed for Texas, where he had inherited property from two sisters, one of whom he promised to marry. He never married her, but he did kill both sisters. He had hoped to build another "Castle" here, but he found that law enforcement officers were more aggressive in Texas than in Chicago, so he headed back east.

In 1894, he and an associate named Benjamin Pitezel made a deal. Pitezel would take out a $10,000 life insurance policy; Holmes would find and disfigure a dead body claim that it was Pitezel, and the two would split the money. Instead, Holmes murdered Pitezel in Philadelphia

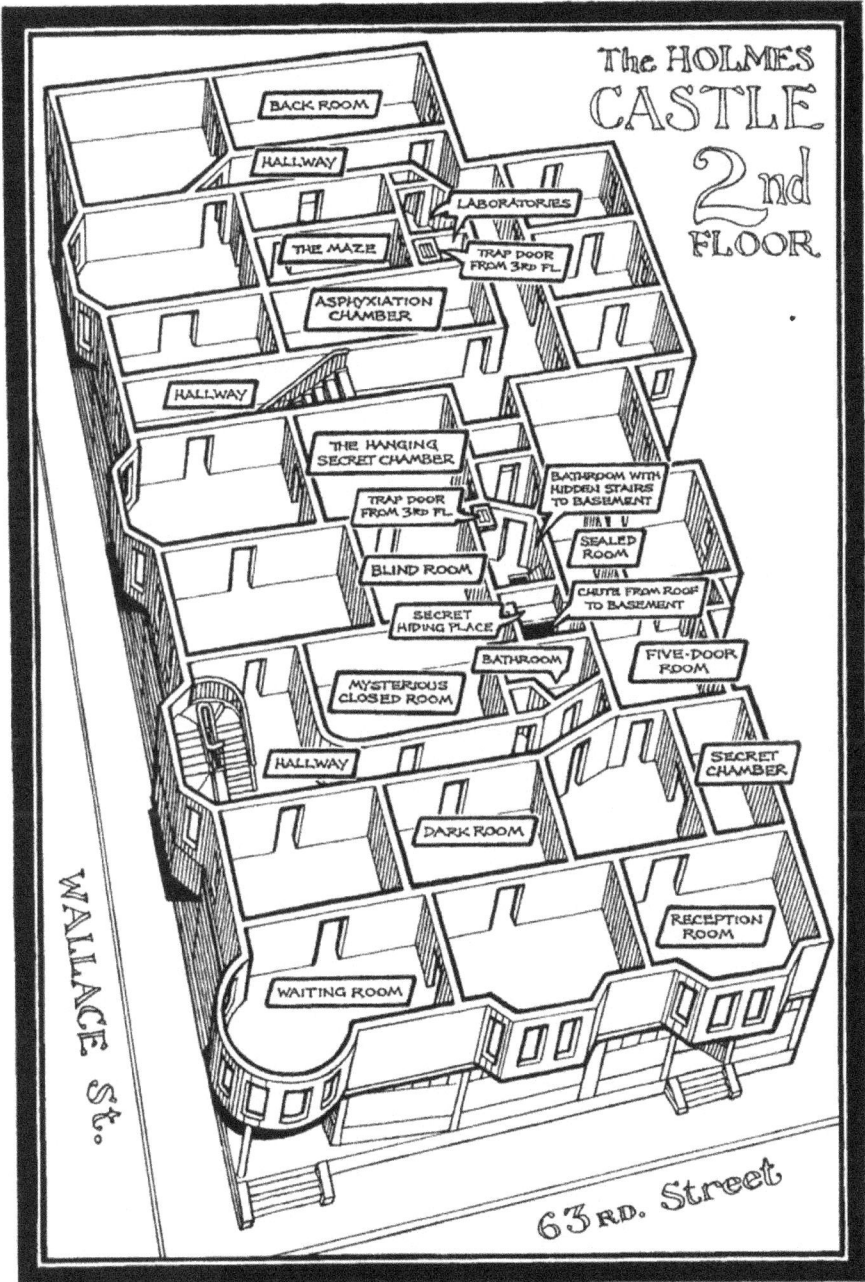

The HOLMES CASTLE 2nd FLOOR

BACK ROOM

HALLWAY

LABORATORIES

THE MAZE

TRAP DOOR FROM 3RD FL.

ASPHYXIATION CHAMBER

HALLWAY

THE HANGING SECRET CHAMBER

BATHROOM WITH HIDDEN STAIRS TO BASEMENT

TRAP DOOR FROM 3RD FL.

SEALED ROOM

BLIND ROOM

CHUTE FROM ROOF TO BASEMENT

SECRET HIDING PLACE

MYSTERIOUS CLOSED ROOM

BATHROOM

FIVE-DOOR ROOM

HALLWAY

SECRET CHAMBER

DARK ROOM

RECEPTION ROOM

WAITING ROOM

WALLACE St.

63RD. Street

125

by burning him alive to support the story of a laboratory accident. He then collected the money himself.

Pitezel had three of his five children with him at the time, and Holmes took the three, a boy and two girls, through the northern United States into Canada. On the way, in Indianapolis, he killed the boy, cut up the body, and burned it. In Toronto, he put the girls into a trunk and gassed them to death. He then buried their bodies in the cellar of the house where he was staying.

Holmes had been jailed for a brief time for his involvement in a horseracing scam before his trip to Canada. While in jail, he told a cellmate about the plan he and Pitezel put together, and he offered the cellmate $500 if he could find a lawyer that would assist Holmes with any legal questions should they arise. The cellmate found the attorney, but Holmes never paid him the $500, and as a result, the cellmate told the police about the Pitezel scam. Holmes was arrested in Boston on November 17, 1894.

Following his arrest, the Chicago police searched the "Castle." In the basement, they found the remains of some of Holmes's victims. They also found evidence that murders had been committed in other rooms in the hotel. Meanwhile, a detective by the name of Frank Geyer was investigating the Pitezel case. He would eventually find the remains of the three children Holmes had killed during his trip to Canada. The public was satisfied that Holmes was a monster.

Holmes was put on trial in Philadelphia for the murder of Pitezel. He was convicted and sentenced to death. After his conviction, he confessed to 30 murders. The Hearst newspapers paid him $7,500 (over $200,000 in today's dollars) for his confession. Holmes went to the gallows on May 7, 1896. The assistant superintendent, a man named Richardson, appeared more nervous than Holmes as he prepared the noose. Holmes turned to him and said, "Take your time, old man." Holmes's neck did not snap, and as a result, he died slowly. He was pronounced dead twenty minutes after the trap had been sprung.

Holmes was buried based on the instructions he left behind. First, cement was poured into the coffin, and then Holmes's body was put in,

The Chicago Tribune *of Sunday, August 18, 1895.*

which was then covered with more cement. His body was then taken to Holy Cross Cemetery just outside of Philadelphia. The grave was dug, and the coffin placed inside. Workers then filled the grave with cement. The grave was left unmarked. Holmes wanted to make sure that neither medical researchers nor relatives of his victims could get to his body.

During his stay in prison, Holmes claimed that the devil possessed him. Events that occurred after his execution caused some to believe it. Detective Geyer became seriously ill. The warden at the Philadelphia prison, where Holmes was held and executed, committed suicide. Accidental electrocution took the life of the foreman of the jury that convicted Holmes. The priest who delivered the last rites to Holmes was found dead on church grounds. Finally, a fire destroyed the office of the Chicago district attorney leaving only a picture of Holmes untouched.

Recently, Jeff Mudgett, Holmes's great-great-grandson, has written a book about his ancestor titled *Bloodstains*. The book provides evidence that Holmes may have been Jack the Ripper. Mudgett notes that there exist records documenting Holmes traveling to London in 1888 to sell skeletons to medical schools. He was not in Chicago when the five murders credited to the Ripper took place. When Holmes returned to Chicago in December of 1888, the Ripper murders stopped. Many believe that the Ripper possessed surgical skills, which Holmes certainly had. Finally, Mudgett had scientists at the University of Buffalo analyze letters written by Jack the Ripper and those written by Holmes while he was in prison. They concluded that the classifier performance number (97.95 percent) indicate that the writings of both men are similar in style. Was America's answer to the Ripper the Ripper himself?

When we visited Holy Cross Cemetery to photograph Holmes's final resting place, we had the section, range, and lot number of the location of the grave. To be sure that our information was accurate, we went to the cemetery office to verify it. The cemetery employee we spoke to told us, "We are not allowed to talk about that grave."

Here is the final resting place of America's first serial killer.

If You Go:
See the "If You Go" section in chapter titled "Philadelphia's Sinners."

17.

EDDIE PLANK

AND

CHRISTY MATHEWSON

"Hall of Fame Hurlers"

Counties: Adams and Union • Towns: Gettysburg and Lewisburg
Plank is buried at Evergreen Cemetery
799 Baltimore Street, Gettysburg
Mathewson is buried at Lewisburg Cemetery
201 South 7th Street, Lewisburg

In 1900 the Bucknell University baseball team took on the Gettysburg nine twice, winning both games. Within two years, a pitcher from both of those teams would begin major league baseball careers that would land them in the Hall of Fame. Both played for Hall of Fame managers, two men who were the best at their profession, John McGraw and Connie Mack (see *Keystone Tombstones Volume One*, Chapter 17). Playing in different leagues, the two never pitched against each other during the regular season, but they made up for that during the World Series. Their names are Christy Mathewson and Eddie Plank, and both are buried in Pennsylvania.

Christy Mathewson was born on August 12, 1880, in Factoryville, Pennsylvania. His mother had hopes that one day he would be a preacher. With that goal in mind, she raised Mathewson in a manner that stressed "regular hours of sleep and plenty of plain, wholesome food, good milk, fresh air, and the Golden Rule." It was not to be, for even at a young age, Mathewson was working on his pitching. He began by tossing silverware out windows because he liked the sound when the objects struck the ground. By the time he was four, he was playing a game called "hailey

Christy Mathewson

over," which involved throwing a ball over a house to an unseen friend who stood on the other side. Mathewson's mother required the child who threw the ball to pay for any broken windows.

Mathewson attended school at the Keystone Academy, where all the members of his family had been educated. Upon graduation, he went to Bucknell University, where he participated in both baseball and football and was elected class president. Mathewson made Walter Camp's All-American Football Team as a drop-kicker in 1900.

130

While attending Bucknell, Mathewson pitched in the minor leagues for two local teams. After leaving college, he signed to play professional baseball in the New England League. In 1900 he signed with Norfolk, a team that played in the Virginia-North Carolina League. He had a very successful season finishing with a record of 20–2. In July of that year, Norfolk sold Mathewson to the New York Giants, and he made six major league appearances that season. He went 0–3 with the Giants and was sent back to Norfolk. The Cincinnati Reds quickly picked up Mathewson from Norfolk and just as promptly turned around and traded him back to the Giants.

Mathewson would have a major league career that spanned seventeen years. During that time, he won 373 games and lost 188. He threw 79 shutouts and retired with an earned run average of 2.13. His win total is still number one in the National League, a distinction he shares with another pitching great, Grover Cleveland Alexander. He struck out 2,507 hitters while walking only 848. Mathewson also threw two no-hitters and won thirty or more games four times. The Giants won five National League titles and one World Series during his career.

Mathewson may not have become a preacher, as his mother had wished, but his upbringing certainly contributed to his behavior as an adult. He was a devout Christian to the point that he refused to pitch on Sundays. According to his mother, he once turned down thousands of dollars, which he would receive for just the use of his name. The offer was refused because his name would be fixed to a Broadway amusement place that offered drinking and dancing. Mathewson also authored a series of children's books and became a role model that parents urged their children to emulate. The great sportswriter Grantland Rice wrote, "Christy Mathewson brought something to baseball that no one else had ever given the game. He played the game with a certain touch of class, an indefinable lift in culture, brains, and personality."

Mathewson retired after the 1916 season. When the United States entered World War I, Mathewson enlisted in the Army. He served in the Chemical Service with another well-known ballplayer by the name of Ty Cobb. He was in France when, during a training exercise, he was accidentally gassed, an incident that led to him developing tuberculosis. When he returned to the United States, he got back into baseball as a coach, and in 1923 he was named part-time president of the Boston Braves. Two years later, on October 7, 1925, the day the World Series began, Mathewson passed away at his home in Saranac Lake, New York. He was buried in the Lewisburg Cemetery in Pennsylvania. In 1936 Mathewson, along with Babe Ruth, Ty Cobb, Walter Johnson, and Honus Wagner, were selected as the first members of the Baseball Hall of Fame.

Edward "Eddie" Plank was born near Gettysburg on August 31, 1875. His parents were farmers, and Plank spent his early life working on their farm. He developed a love for the game of baseball, and it has been said that his first backstop was a haystack. Along with friends, he formed a baseball team that soon became known as one of the best in Adams County. This was largely because Plank was the team's pitcher. When he was 25, the Gettysburg College baseball coach had him enroll at the Gettysburg Academy, which made him eligible to play for the college team. For two years, he pitched for Gettysburg so effectively that he was noticed by a man named Cornelius McGillicuddy, who was better known as Connie Mack. Mack signed Plank to play on his professional team, the Philadelphia Athletics.

Plank made his major league debut on May 13, 1901. In his rookie year, he went 17–13. During his seventeen-year career, he established himself as one of the greatest pitchers in major league history. It can be argued that Plank was the best left-handed pitcher ever to play the game until Warren Spahn came along. He won 20 or more games in a season seven times. His career record was 326–194, with an earned run average of 2.35. He also recorded 2,246 strikeouts. He played with the Athletics through the 1914 season and was a major contributor to that team, winning six American League titles and three World Series. He ended his career in 1917, playing for the St. Louis Browns. He was 42 years old when he hung up his spikes. Plank's teammate, Hall of Fame second baseman Eddie Collins, said, "Plank was not the fastest, not the trickiest, not the possessor of the most stuff, but he was just the greatest." In 1946, Plank was inducted into the Baseball Hall of Fame.

Eddie Plank

After he retired, Plank returned to Gettysburg, where he ran a car dealership. He talked about returning to the family farm, but that was not to be. On February 25, 1926, Plank suffered a stroke and died. He was just 50 years old. Plank was laid to rest in the Evergreen Cemetery located in Gettysburg. His obituary stated that while in college, he pitched against Christy Mathewson on two occasions. This was not the case as Plank didn't pitch for Gettysburg until after Mathewson began playing minor league baseball. However, they were on opposite sides in three World Series (1905, 1911, and 1913.)

The 1905 World Series opened on October the 9th in Philadelphia at Columbia Park. It marked the first time fans got the chance to see Christy Mathewson pitch against Eddie Plank. The paying customers got their money's worth as the game turned into a pitcher's duel. Neither team scored until the top of the fifth when Mathewson started things off with a single. He was forced out at second by Roger Bresnahan, who made up for it by stealing that base. The next batter flied out, but then Mike Donlin singled to left scoring Bresnahan, and Donlin took second on the throw to the plate. The next batter walked, and Sam Mertes followed that with a double that scored Donlin. The Giants scored another run in the ninth, and Mathewson emerged victorious by pitching a four-hit shutout.

The second game of the series was played the following day at the Polo Grounds in New York and matched two more future Hall of Fame pitchers. The Athletics sent Chief Bender to the mound to face the Giants' 21-game winner, Joe McGinnity. The Athletics scored an unearned run in the third and added two earned runs in the eighth inning. Bender pitched magnificently and emerged a winner by a score of 3–0.

Two days later, the series moved back to Philadelphia, where John McGraw once again sent Christy Mathewson to the mound, this time to face the Athletics' Andy Coakley. The Giants jumped on Coakley for two runs in the first and five more in the fifth. Meanwhile, Mathewson continued to shut down the Athletics, not allowing a runner to reach third base. The Giants added two runs in the ninth to win 9–0, and Mathewson pitched another four-hit shutout.

The 1905 World Series at the Polo Grounds.

Game Four moved back to the Polo Grounds and was played on Friday, October 13th. Plank took the mound where Joe McGinnity would oppose him. If anyone had bad luck this Friday the 13th, it was the hitters on both teams. In the fourth inning, the Giants scored an unearned run. It would be the only run scored in the game. Both Plank and McGinnity pitched five hitters, but the Giants won 1–0 and now led the series three games to one.

Game Five took place the next day at the Polo Grounds. Mathewson once again was named the Giants' starter, and this time he would face Chief Bender. The game was scoreless until the bottom of the fifth when the Giants scored a single run. They added an insurance run in the eighth. Mathewson wrapped up the series by getting the three Athletic batters in the ninth on ground outs. He again pitched a shutout, this time giving up only five hits. Mathewson's World Series performance made him a nationwide hero. He had pitched three shutouts and only allowed one Athletic to get as far as third base. Mathewson's 1905 World Series performance has never been duplicated. Athletic manager Connie Mack may have been thinking back to this performance when he said of Mathewson, "It was wonderful to watch him pitch when he wasn't pitching against you."

Mathewson's Giants faced Plank's Athletics once again in the 1911 World Series, though the two would not pitch against each other. Mathewson knew this was an entirely different team than the one he faced in 1905, so he contacted American League players he knew to obtain data on the batters he would face. He later wrote that this research aided him in the series.

The 1911 Athletics were indeed a different outfit than the team the Giants beat in 1905. They fielded what was called the "$100,000 infield" that was led by future Hall of Famers Frank Baker and Eddie Collins. They had won 102 regular season games behind a solid pitching staff that included Jack Coombs, who went 28–12; Plank, who posted a 22–8 record; and Chief Bender, who ended the regular season at 17–5. The Giants were a team featuring speed. As a team, they set the major league record by stealing 347 bases. Their pitching staff was solid as well, led by Mathewson, who had gone 26–13; and Rube Marquard, who went 24–7.

Game One was played on Saturday, October 14th, at a newly-constructed Polo Grounds (the prior stadium had burned to the ground early in the year). The game attracted a record-breaking crowd of 38,281 who came to watch Mathewson oppose Chief Bender. As expected, the game turned into a pitcher's duel. The Athletics finally scored a run on Mathewson in the second inning when Frank Baker scored on a single hit by Harry Davis. The Giants tied the game in the fourth and took the lead in the seventh when Chief Meyers scored on a double hit by Josh Devore. Mathewson didn't give up another run as he pitched a six-hitter in the Giants 2–1 victory.

Game Two took place the following Monday at Shibe Park in Philadelphia. This one matched Plank against the Giants' Rube Marquard. As might be expected, the game was a low-scoring affair, and base runners were hard to come by. The game was tied at one apiece in the bottom of the sixth, and Marquard had retired 13 Athletics in a row. With two outs, Eddie Collins came to the plate and lashed a double to left field. Frank Baker was the next hitter, and the count reached 1–1. Marquard later described what happened next:

> When he came up in the sixth, I fully intended to follow instructions and give him curved balls. But when I had one strike on him and when he refused to bite on another outcurve which was a little too wide, I thought to cross him by sending in a fast-high ball the kind I knew he liked.

Baker liked the pitch because he smashed it over the right-field fence giving the Athletics a 3–1 lead. That proved to be the final score, and Eddie Plank had won his first World Series game.

Mathewson also had a story about Game Two. His teammate, Josh Devore, had run into Ty Cobb, and he questioned the great hitter on Eddie Plank. Devore told Mathewson that Cobb knew all about hitting and what to expect from Eddie Plank. Devore also told Mathewson that he couldn't wait to face Plank. Devore did face him, and he struck out four times. After the game, Mathewson said to Devore, "I thought you

Newspaper from the 1911 World Series Game 3 – Mathewson on left, Combs on right.

knew all about that fellow." Devore responded that he had learned that Cobb and Plank were friends and "I guess Ty was giving me a bad steer."

Game Three was held the following day back at the new Polo Grounds. The Athletics sent Jack Coombs to the mound to face Christy Mathewson. Going into the ninth inning, Mathewson and the Giants had a 1–0 lead. Frank Baker came to the plate. Mathewson was confident he had the game in hand, but Baker had other ideas, and in short order, the Giant pitcher was watching yet another ball sail out of the park off Baker's bat. This one was significant because, after the blast, he became known as "Home Run Baker." The game went eleven innings, and the Athletics finally beat Mathewson by a score of 3–2. Both pitchers went the distance.

Game Four was delayed a full week due to the weather. Finally, on October 24th, the two teams took the field at Shibe Park in Philadelphia. With a full week of rest, Mathewson was sent to the mound to face Chief Bender. The Giants jumped off to a 2–0 lead in the first. Mathewson pitched well through three innings, but the Athletics got to him, scoring three runs in the fourth. In the fifth Baker doubled home Collins and Philadelphia had a 4–2 lead. After giving up those two runs in the first, Chief Bender shut out the Giants the rest of the way giving Philadelphia a lead of 3 games to 1 in the series.

The Polo Grounds was the site for Game Five, and McGraw sent Rube Marquard out to face Jack Coombs. In the top of the third, Philadelphia center fielder Rube Oldring smashed a three-run homer. McGraw pinch-hit for Marquard in the bottom of that inning, which took him out of the game. Coombs shut out the Giants until the seventh when they scored a single run. It was still 3–1 going into the bottom of the ninth. The Athletics were three outs away from winning the series. Coombs retired the first batter, but the Giants' Fletcher followed with a double. The next batter grounded out, bringing up Doc Crandall the Giants' pitcher. McGraw let him hit, and he responded with a double that drove in a run. Devore singled Crandall home, sending the game into extra innings. Coombs was up second in the tenth, and he beat out a bunt, but he pulled a groin muscle and had to be replaced. Crandall then retired the side, and Connie Mack brought Plank in as his relief pitcher. Doyle, the Giant second baseman, got things started by hitting a double. The next batter bunted, and Plank attempted to throw Doyle out at third, but the runner slid in safely. Doyle then scored on a sacrifice fly giving the Giants the win and keeping them alive in the series.

Game Six was played back at Shibe Park, and McGraw selected Red Ames to pitch against Chief Bender. By the end of the sixth inning, Philadelphia had a 6–1 lead. The home team added seven more runs in the seventh, putting the game out of reach. The final score was 13–2, and the Athletics were the World Champions.

The 1913 World Series once again featured the New York Giants and the Philadelphia Athletics. In this series, Mathewson and Plank would face each other twice. The Giants appeared in their third consecutive series, having lost to Philadelphia in 1911 and Boston in 1912. Giant Manager John McGraw received heavy criticism after the 1912 series over the way he handled his pitchers. He was very determined to beat Connie Mack's club in 1913.

Game One was played on October 7th in New York at the Polo grounds. The Athletics sent Chief Bender to the mound to face Rube Marquard. Philadelphia's Home Run Baker was the hero in this contest driving in three runs on three hits that included a home run. Philadelphia won 6–4 and took the series lead.

The next day the two teams played Game Two at Shibe Park in Philadelphia. This game featured Mathewson versus Plank, and as many expected, the bats for both teams were quieted. After nine innings, the score was still 0–0, and the game went into extra innings. In the top of the tenth, the Giants scored three times with Mathewson driving in the first run with a single. Mathewson retired the Athletics in the bottom of the inning, pitching yet another shutout and tying up the series.

In Game Three, played at the Polo Grounds, Connie Mack sent rookie Bullet Joe Bush into pitch against Jeff Tesreau. Philadelphia scored five runs in the first two innings. Bush gave up single runs to the Giants in the fifth and seventh innings as Philadelphia took a 2–1 series lead by a winning score of 8–2.

Scene from Game 3 of the 1913 World Series at the Polo Grounds.

On Friday, October 10th, the two teams returned to Shibe Park in Philadelphia. Chief Bender was on the mound for the Athletics, and through five innings, he was coasting along with a 6–0 lead. The Giants roared back in the seventh when Fred Merkle launched a three-run homer. The visitors scored two more in the eighth to make the score 6–5. Bender recovered and retired the side in the ninth, giving him his fourth straight series win. Philadelphia was a win away from claiming the championship.

The next day the two teams took the field at the Polo Grounds. Mathewson was back on the mound, where he would face Plank for the second time in the series. Mathewson pitched well, giving up three runs on just six hits. Plank on this day threw a masterful two-hitter leading his team to another World Series Championship by a score of 3–1. It was the last time the two great pitchers would ever face each other.

Baseball honors continued to be bestowed on the two Pennsylvania pitchers long after they passed away. In 1999, *The Sporting News* ranked Mathewson number 7 on their list of the 100 greatest baseball players. ESPN selected his play in the 1905 World Series as the greatest playoff performance of all time. *The Sporting News* ranked Plank 68th on that same list, and he was nominated for the Major League Baseball All-Century Team.

Both Mathewson and Plank are mentioned in the Ogden Nash poem "Line-Up for Yesterday." Of Mathewson, Nash wrote:

M is for Matty,
Who carried a charm
In the form of an extra
Brain in his arm.

Regarding Plank, he wrote:

P is for Plank,
The arm of the A's;
When he tangled with Matty
Games lasted for days.

Here lies a man who some still consider to be the greatest pitcher in the history of baseball.

Here is the grave of Hall of Fame pitcher Eddie Plank. Note the grave goods left to honor the southpaw who has been dead since 1926.

If You Go:

Should you decide to visit Christy Mathewson at Lewisburg Cemetery, you may want to pay your respects at a couple of other graves. Congressional Medal of Honor recipient George Henry Ramer was laid to rest in the cemetery. Ramer was awarded the nation's highest military award for his actions on September 12, 1951, during the Korean War. Ramer led an attack on an enemy-held hilltop position. During the attack, he and most of his men were wounded. Though he and his men were facing machine gun, mortar, and arms fire, they were successful in destroying an enemy bunker and capturing the position. The enemy quickly launched a counterattack, and Ramer ordered his men to withdraw while he fought to cover their escape. Though wounded a second time, he refused aid and ordered the remaining men to continue to withdraw. He continued to fight until he was fatally wounded.

One of baseball's great pinch hitters, Henry "Moose" McCormick is also buried in the Lewisburg Cemetery. He played for the New York Giants and the Pittsburgh Pirates in 1904. In 1908, he split a season playing for the Philadelphia Phillies and the New York Giants. He ended his career with the Giants in 1913. He retired with a lifetime batting average of .285.

In 1908, while playing for the Giants, McCormick was a key player in the infamous Merkle game. That game was played on September 23, 1908, and matched the Giants against the Chicago Cubs, two teams that were fighting to win the National League pennant. The Giants came to bat in the bottom of the ninth with the score tied at 1–1. With two outs, McCormick lined a single to left field. Fred Merkle then came to the plate and delivered a hit down the right-field line. McCormick raced to third, and Merkle stopped at first. Al Bridwell came to the plate and lined a hit to right-center, bringing McCormick home with what should have been the winning run. Fans rushed the field to celebrate, and Merkle was halfway to second base when he turned and ran for the safety of the Giant's clubhouse. A Chicago player by the name of Johnny Evers saw that Merkle failed to touch second base. He called for the ball, and the umpire ruled that Merkle had been forced out, negating the winning run. The game ended in a tie, and at season's end, the Cubs and Giants were tied for first place. A one-game playoff was held, and the Cubs won. Had McCormick's run counted, no playoff would have been needed, and the Giants would have won the pennant.

After visiting Lewisburg Cemetery, we went in search of a place to have lunch. We found the Bull Run Inn located at 605 Market Street. Lewisburg is a college town, and this was very much a college place advertising all-day drink specials. The Inn also offers a wide variety of domestic and imported beers. Our food was good and reasonably priced. If you make the trip, you might want to check this place out.

Should you decide to visit Eddie Plank, you will be in the historically rich town of Gettysburg. While at Evergreen Cemetery, you may also want to check out the graves of John Burns (see *Keystone Tombstones Volume One*, Chapter 4) and Ginnie Wade (see *Keystone Tombstones Volume One*, Chapter 28). You can find plenty of other important historical sites on your visit.

For refreshments, we highly recommend a stop at Gettysburg Eddie's. This is a terrific place loaded with information and memorabilia relating to Eddie Plank. The menu is varied, and the food is excellent. You might also want some liquid refreshments, and the place can answer your every need. Eddie's is located at 217 Steinwehr Avenue.

The authors enjoying some liquid refreshments at Gettysburg Eddie's.

18.

FRED ROGERS

"America's Favorite Neighbor"

County: Westmoreland • Town: Latrobe
Buried at Unity Cemetery
114 Chapel Lane

Fred Rogers was an American treasure and icon. He had a profound effect on the lives of millions of people through his ministry to children and families. His message was simple; that you can be lovable just the way you are. He taught kindness and love over four decades through his television program, books, and songs. He helped children deal with common fears, such as starting school or going to the doctor. He became an American icon of children's entertainment and education as well as a symbol of compassion, patience, and morality. He received the Presidential Medal of Freedom, two Peabody Awards for his life's work, and was inducted into the Television Hall of Fame.

It all began in Latrobe, Pennsylvania, where Fred McFeely Rogers was born on March 20, 1928. He showed an early interest and aptitude for music fostered by his mother and maternal grandfather, Fred McFeely. He graduated from Latrobe High School and attended Dartmouth College before transferring to Rollins College in Florida, where he graduated with a degree in music in 1951.

He was fascinated with the new medium, television, so he put his plans to become a minister on a back burner and accepted a job with NBC in New York City. He worked on several shows but grew disillusioned and left to help found WQED, the nation's first community-supported public television station. He married his college sweetheart, Sara Joanne Byrd, moved back to the Pittsburgh area, and began working at WQED.

Fred Rogers

He developed *The Children's Corner,* a prototype for *Mister Rogers' Neighborhood* and, for the next several years, developed many of the puppets, characters, and music used in his later work, such as King Friday XIII, Daniel Striped Tiger, and X the Owl. During this time, Rogers was studying theology at nearby Pittsburgh Theological Seminary and was ordained a Presbyterian minister in 1962. That year he created a fifteen-minute version of *Mister Rogers' Neighborhood* for Canadian television, and in 1966, WQED launched the series as a half-hour show. In 1969, *Mister Rogers' Neighborhood* began airing on PBS stations across the United States.

Mister Rogers' Neighborhood was a carefully structured show. The routine of walking through the door and changing his sneakers and sweater was a ritual designed to give children a sense of security and to signal a time for a relaxed visit together. The trips between fantasy and reality had structured transitions, such as the summoning of the Neighborhood Trolley to take us from Mister Rogers's living room through a tunnel and into the Neighborhood of Make-Believe. Songs composed by Rogers, more than 200 in his career, were used to impart many of his messages through simple lyrics that speak to a child's concerns. Songs like Daniel Striped Tiger's "Sometimes I Wonder If I'm a Mistake" say it's okay for kids to be themselves, and "What Do You Do?" offers a list of ways for a child to deal with anger.

Typically, each week's episode explored a major theme, such as going to school for the first time or a visit to the hospital to show children what to expect. The program became a huge success. From 1968 to 1999, 895 episodes were produced, all of which Rogers wrote and executive produced. Often there were celebrity guests like Yo-Yo Ma, Tony Bennett, Julia Child, Lynn Swann, David Copperfield, and Pittsburgh native actor Michael Keaton who also worked on the show as a stagehand.

The popularity of the show and its repetitive format led to many parodies over the years. After Burger King used an actor impersonating Mister Rogers for a TV commercial ("Can you say, 'Flame-Broiled'? I knew you could"), Fred Rogers called the head of the company concerned that the ad was "confusing innocent children" into thinking he was promoting their fast-food franchises. Rogers never did any commercial promotions of any kind. Burger King openly apologized, and the commercial was pulled. Johnny Carson once did a skit on *The Tonight Show* called "Mister Rambo's Neighborhood." When Rogers complained, Carson apologized and expressed admiration for Rogers's work. Rogers did, however, have a good sense of humor and enjoyed Eddie Murphy's parody of his show on *Saturday Night Live* called "Mister Robinson's Neighborhood" ("Can you say, 'Eviction Notice'? I knew you could.")

Rogers also published many books to supplement the messages on his television show. Among these were *Mister Rogers Talks with Parents*, *You are Special*, *The World According to Mister Rogers*, *Important Things to Remember*, and eight New Experiences titles such as *The New Baby*, *Moving*, and *When a Pet Dies*.

In 1968, Rogers was appointed Chairman of the Forum on Mass Media and Child Development of the White House Conference on Youth. In 1969 he appeared before the United States Senate in support of funding for PBS and the Corporation for Public Broadcasting. He spoke on the need for social and emotional education that public television provided and argued that alternative television programming helped encourage children to become happy and productive citizens, sometimes opposing fewer positive messages in the media and popular culture. He even recited lyrics to "What Do You Do?" The chairman of the subcommittee, Senator John Pastore, said the testimony had given him goosebumps. President Nixon had proposed cutting their budget to $9 million, but after Rogers's testimony, Congress agreed on $22 million.

In 1979, Rogers testified in the case *Sony Corp of America v. Universal City Studios Inc.* The Supreme Court considered his testimony and quoted him in the footnote in its decision that held that the Betamax video recorder did not infringe copyright.

At the 1998 Emmy's, Rogers was awarded the Lifetime Achievement Award. In accepting the award on stage, he said, "All of us have special ones who have loved us into being. Would you just take, along with me, ten seconds to think of the people who have helped you become who you are. Ten seconds of silence." The gesture brought many of the star-studded Hollywood crowd to

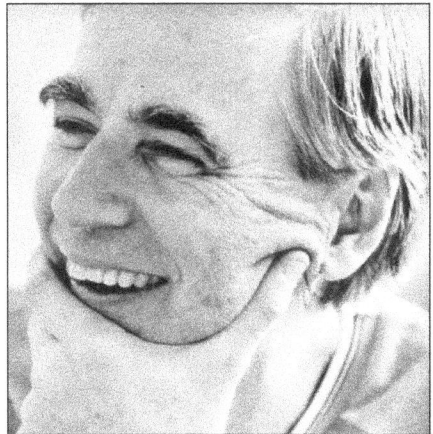

Photo of Fred Rogers located at the Rogers Center on the campus of Saint Vincent's College in Latrobe.

This large statue of Fred Rogers sits just outside Heinz Field in Pittsburgh. The site is called Tribute to Children.

tears and drew a standing ovation. After that, Rogers frequently repeated this in his many speeches and appearances.

Production of *Mister Rogers' Neighborhood* ceased in December 1999 and the last week of original episodes aired in August 2000. After the production of the program ceased, Fred Rogers devoted his time to the *Mister Rogers' Neighborhood* website, writing books, and numerous speaking engagements.

Rogers was diagnosed with stomach cancer in December 2002. His last public appearance was as Grand Marshall of the Tournament of Roses Parade with Bill Cosby and Art Linkletter. He died on February 27, 2003, at his home with his wife by his side. He was just shy of 75 years old.

He never sought the spotlight, but the list of awards he was presented is enormous. The Presidential Medal of Freedom, the highest civilian award that can be bestowed, was awarded Rogers in 2002 by President George Bush. *Mister Rogers' Neighborhood* won four Emmy Awards, and

Rogers was given a Lifetime Achievement Award by the Academy of Television Arts and Sciences. He was awarded two Peabody Awards, was named one of the "50 greatest TV stars of all time" by *TV Guide* in 1996, was inducted into the Television Hall of Fame in 1999, had an asteroid named after him (Misterrogers), and got a star on the Hollywood Walk of Fame. The Smithsonian Institution in Washington, D.C., has his signature sweater on display. There is a large memorial statue of Fred Rogers just outside of Heinz Field, and St. Vincent College in Latrobe is home to The Fred M. Rogers Center for Early Learning and Children's Media. In 2003, the U.S. House of Representatives unanimously passed Resolution 111 honoring Rogers for "his legendary service to the improvement of lives of children, his steadfast commitment to demonstrating the power of compassion, and his dedication to spreading kindness through example."

Fred Rogers was a soft-spoken man of great modesty with a steady hand and a generous heart. His television persona was no act. This author had the privilege of meeting him several times and even seeing him

Fred Rogers was laid to rest in this mausoleum in Latrobe, Pennsylvania.

record an episode of *Mister Rogers' Neighborhood*. He was always patient, caring, humble, and kind to everyone. He is buried in historic Unity Cemetery in Latrobe, Pennsylvania, in a mausoleum that does not bear his name. It has the name "Given," a relative of Rogers.

If You Go:

If you go to Latrobe, be sure to visit the beautiful, inspiring campus of the community of scholars known as St. Vincent College. Established in 1846, it has been turning out some of our best thinkers for over 150 years (This author went there). It's also the training camp of the Pittsburgh Steelers. If that's not enough stimulation, stop at Sharky's Café at 3960 Rt 30. Sharky's has been turning out some of our best drinkers for many years. It's the area's largest and most complete restaurant and sports bar. Even President Obama and Senator Bob Casey stopped in for a beer when campaigning in the area. It's a festive, friendly atmosphere. We loved it.

19.

BESSIE SMITH

"The Empress of the Blues"

County: Delaware • Town: Sharon Hill
Buried at Mount Lawn Cemetery
84th Street and Hook Road

Bob Dylan and the Band recorded an album in 1967 titled *The Basement Tapes*. The record was released until 1975. One of the tracks is a song composed by Band members Robbie Robertson and Rick Danko on which Dylan provides the lead vocal. When he gets to the chorus, he sings:

> I'm just going down the road to see Bessie.
> Oh, see her soon.
> Going down the road to see Bessie Smith.
> When I get there, I wonder what she'll do.

The song is called "Bessie Smith," and it pays homage to a woman that many consider to be the greatest blues singer of all time. Smith is buried in Sharon Hill, Pennsylvania, not far from Philadelphia.

According to the 1900 census, Bessie Smith was born in Chattanooga, Tennessee, in July 1892. When the 1910 census was recorded, her birth date changed to April 15, 1894. The latter date is the one she observed throughout her life. By the time Smith was nine, both of her parents had died, and as a result, she was raised by an older sister. She was raised in poverty, and to bring some money into the household, Smith and one of her brothers formed a duo and began performing on the streets of Chattanooga. She would sing and dance to the music her brother supplied on his guitar.

Bessie Smith

In 1912 she auditioned for a job in a traveling show known as the Stokes troupe. She was hired as a dancer because the show already had a woman singer named Ma Rainey. Many believe that Ma Rainey helped Smith as she grew to become a stage performer. By 1913 she had developed her act, and by 1920 she was well known throughout the South.

In 1920 a singer by the name of Mamie Smith (no relation) recorded and released a song titled "Crazy Blues." It turned out to be a hit and prompted the recording industry to search for other female blues singers. In 1923, Smith signed a recording contract with Columbia Records. By that time, she had made Philadelphia her home and met and married Jack Gee, a security guard. By all accounts, the marriage was rocky from the start with both partners having affairs. Gee couldn't come to terms with Smith's bisexuality, and when she learned that he was having an affair with another singer, she ended the relationship in 1929. Smith would eventually enter a common-law marriage with Richard Morgan, who happened to be Lionel Hampton's uncle. Their relationship would endure until the day she died.

While her personal life wasn't going well, Smith's professional career could hardly have been improved upon. Her first record, called "Downhearted Blues," was a major hit. She became the highest-paid black performer in the 1920s as she headed her show that featured as many as forty other entertainers. While touring, she lived and traveled in her private railroad car. Columbia Records called her the "Queen of the Blues," but newspapers gave her the upgraded title "Empress."

Smith was known for her powerful voice that was excellent for recording. She recorded more than 150 songs for Columbia backed by some of the greatest musicians at the time, including Joe Smith, Fletcher Henderson, and a young fellow by the name of Louis Armstrong. Her career was cut short by the Great Depression and the advent of talking movies. The first event almost ended the entire recording industry, and "talkies" pretty much ended vaudeville shows.

In 1929, Smith appeared in the film *St. Louis Blues*. She sang the title song in the movie accompanied by Fletcher Henderson's band, a choir, and a string section. The combination produced a sound very different from anything found on her recordings.

In the early thirties, Smith continued to tour and perform. In 1933, John Hammond had her record for Okeh Records. She was paid $37.50 for each recording. Music had entered the swing era, and she was backed by notable swing era musicians including pianist Buck Washington, tenor saxophonist Chu Berry, and guitarist Bobby Johnson. This recording session, which took place on November 24th, would be her last.

Billie Holiday, who cited Smith as a major influence, would make her first record three days later with these same musicians.

On September 26, 1937, Smith was traveling in a car, driven by Richard Morgan, on Route 61 between Memphis, Tennessee, and Clarksdale, Mississippi. Morgan failed to properly judge the speed of a truck that was ahead of him. He attempted to avoid hitting the truck by passing it on the left but was not successful as he hit the rear of the truck with the passenger side of his vehicle. Smith, sitting in the passenger seat, was badly hurt; Morgan had no injuries.

A Memphis surgeon by the name of Dr. Hugh Smith and his fishing partner, Henry Broughton, came upon the accident scene and stopped to help. Dr. Smith examined the injured singer and concluded that she had lost about a half-pint of blood and that her right arm was almost completely severed at the elbow. Broughton and Dr. Smith moved Smith to the side of the road, where he dressed the arm injury while Broughton went to a nearby home to summon an ambulance.

By the time Broughton returned to the scene, Smith was in shock. As time passed, with no ambulance arriving, Dr. Smith decided to take Smith to a hospital in his car. He had just finished clearing out his back seat when he heard a car approaching at a high rate of speed. The fast-moving car hit the doctor's vehicle sending it into Smith's car, demolishing it. The oncoming car went into a ditch on the right side of the road, barely missing Broughton and Bessie Smith.

The ambulance finally arrived, and Smith was taken to Clarksdale's G.T. Thomas Afro-American Hospital. Her right arm was amputated, but she remained in a coma. She died later that morning, having never regained consciousness. After her death, John Hammond circulated a rumor that she had died after being refused entrance to a whites-only hospital. This was not the case, for as Dr. Smith noted, no ambulance driver in the South at that time "would even have thought of putting a colored person off in a hospital for white folks."

Smith's body was placed in the O.V. Catto Elks Lodge to handle the crowd who came to wish her farewell. It is estimated that 10,000 people

*This tombstone partially paid for by Janis Joplin marks
Bessie Smith's final resting place.*

filed past her coffin. She was laid to rest in Mount Lawn Cemetery on
October 4, 1937. Though money was raised for a tombstone to mark her
grave, her estranged husband, Jack Gee, pocketed the money, and Smith's
grave remained unmarked until August 7, 1970. On that day, a tombstone
partially paid for by Janis Joplin was erected. Joplin also recorded a song
called "Stone for Bessie Smith" on her album *Mythical Kings and Iguanas*.

Three of Bessie Smith's recordings have been inducted into the
Grammy Hall of Fame. The songs "Downhearted Blues," "St. Louis
Blues," and "Empty Bed Blues" were recognized for their historical signifi-
cance. "Downhearted Blues" is also in the Rock and Roll Hall of Fame,
having been selected as one of the 500 songs that shaped that genre of
music. Smith herself was inducted into the Rock and Roll Hall of Fame in
1989. She is also a member of the Blues Hall of Fame and the Big Band
and Jazz Hall of Fame.

Several great female vocalists have acknowledged that Smith influenced them. These include Billie Holiday, Sarah Vaughn, Aretha
Franklin, and Janis Joplin, who said of Smith, "She showed me the air
and taught me how to fill it."

Of course, her influence has not been confined to female singers. As
noted at the beginning of this chapter, Bob Dylan and the Band have

also paid tribute to the great blues singer in the song "Bessie Smith." As Dylan sings in the songs last verse:

> When she sees me, will she know what I've been through?
> Will old times start to feeling like new?
> When I get there, will our love still feel so true?
> Yet all I have; I'll be bringing it to you
> Oh Bessie, sing them old-time blues.

If You Go:

Mount Lawn Cemetery is the final resting place of another entertainer, Lawrence Brown Sr., who was a vocalist with Harold Melvin and the Blue Notes. In the 1970s, this popular group had hits with several songs including, "The Love I Lost," "If You Don't Know Me by Now," and "Wake Up Everybody." Brown performed until a few months before his death in 2008.

Hank "The Bankman" Gathers is also buried in this cemetery. Gathers was a college basketball star who became the second player in the history of the game to lead the nation in both scoring and rebounding. He died during a game on March 4, 1990. The cause of his death was heart failure.

Another basketball player, Guy Rodgers, was also laid to rest at Mount Lawn. Rodgers had a 12-year career as a guard in the National Basketball Association. During that time, he played for the San Francisco Warriors, the Chicago Bulls, the Cincinnati Royals, and the Milwaukee Bucks. Rodgers passed away in 2001.

Not far from Mount Lawn is the town of Essington, Pennsylvania. We stopped for refreshments at Coaches Bar and Grille, located at 350 Jansen Avenue. The food was excellent and reasonably priced. There are a large outdoor patio and numerous televisions for your viewing pleasure. The wait staff was friendly, courteous, and efficient. If you are in the area, we recommend a visit.

20.

THADDEUS STEVENS

"The Dictator of Congress"

County: Lancaster • Town: Lancaster
Buried at Shreiner-Concord Cemetery
Mulberry and West Chester Streets

There have been many powerful congressmen who have served in the United States House of Representatives. A majority have held the title Speaker of the House. Members who have held that lofty position include Henry Clay, Champ Clark, Sam Rayburn, and Tip O'Neill. However, only one member of the House was ever called "The Dictator of Congress." His name was Thaddeus Stevens, and many historians hold the opinion that he wielded more power than any other congressman in the history of the country.

Stevens was born on April 4, 1792, in Vermont. He faced numerous hardships in his early life, including a club foot. Also, his father was an alcoholic who found it impossible to hold a steady job. It is not known what happened to the elder Stevens, but he left his wife and four sons in poverty. Stevens himself was ambitious and saw the value of education. He studied at Peacham Academy and afterward entered Dartmouth as a sophomore from where he graduated in 1814. Stevens then moved to York, Pennsylvania, where he worked as a teacher while he studied law. He was admitted to the bar and established himself first as a lawyer in Gettysburg and later in Lancaster.

Stevens would never marry, though he did have two boys, who were the sons of his mixed-race housekeeper, Lydia Hamilton Smith, who lived with him, and would be considered a common-law wife by today's standards. Smith would manage Stevens's home and businesses

Thaddeus Stevens

in Lancaster for 24 years. She also served as his hostess during his days in Washington. During this time, society operated under a policy of segregation. As a result, rumors swirled about their relationship. Based on their correspondence and accounts by those who knew them, it appears that the relationship they established could best be described at the time as a respectful friendship.

Stevens was deeply interested in politics. Initially, he joined the Federalist Party. When that party faded, he joined the Anti-Masonic Party. He then became a Whig before finding his final home as a Republican. In 1833 he was elected to the Pennsylvania State House of Representatives, where he served on and off until 1842. His record during this time reflects beliefs he would carry forward throughout his political career. He was against secret societies, he favored funding to Pennsylvania colleges, and he wanted a constitutional limit established on the state debt. His support for black citizens surfaced when he refused to sign the Pennsylvania Constitution of 1838 because it failed to allow those citizens to vote. He also championed the establishment of free public schools. Though Stevens had been elected by a constituency that favored repeal of the public education act, he fought to preserve it. He was instrumental in persuading the Pennsylvania Assembly to vote overwhelmingly in favor of keeping the new law.

Those who knew Stevens agreed that he was a man who could be counted on to employ his considerable energies toward furthering those causes in which he believed. It was his view that slave owners were attempting to gain control of the federal government to ensure that slavery would be permitted to grow. He vowed to fight to further the cause of liberty. He was first elected to Congress in 1848, and he served until 1853. In 1859 he returned to Congress as a Republican and continued to serve until his death in 1868. As a member of Congress, he supported Native Americans, Mormons, Jews, and women. However, no cause was dearer to him than that of the abolition of slavery. He was an active member of the Underground Railroad, and he assisted in helping runaway slaves make their way to Canada. A possible Underground Railroad site has been discovered under his office in Lancaster, Pennsylvania.

When the Civil War broke out, Stevens used his political skills to enhance his influence and power. He became the chairman of the Ways and Means Committee, and combining the power of this position with his oratorical skills, he soon became the leader of a group that would be known as the Radical Republicans.

Stevens was outraged in July of 1861 when Congress passed the Crittenden-Johnson Resolution, which held that the war would be won by restoring the Union while preserving slavery. Stevens worked hard for its repeal, which occurred that December. In that same month, he was calling for the emancipation of the slaves to weaken the Confederate States. In early 1862 he was calling for total war. On January 22nd he addressed the House and declared that the war would not end until, ". . . one party or the other be reduced to hopeless feebleness, and the power of further effort shall be utterly annihilated." In that same speech, he again urged the immediate emancipation of all slaves, arguing that such a move would assist in crippling the Confederate economy that relied on slave labor to raise cotton, rice, tobacco, and grain.

That January, Lincoln also acted within his cabinet. He appointed his embattled Secretary of War, Simon Cameron (see *Keystone Tombstones Volume One*, Chapter 5), to the post of United States Minister to Russia. Upon hearing this news, Stevens said, "Send word to the Czar to bring in his things of the night." Besides, before his departure to Russia, the House censured Cameron for adopting policies that flagrantly damaged the public service.

By the time the war was ending, Stevens was the acknowledged leader of the Radical Republicans. The elections of 1866 put this group in firm control of the Congress. Stevens became the architect of the country's policies governing the Reconstruction of the Southern states. He planned to use military power to force the South to recognize the equality of the freed slaves. Lincoln's successor, President Andrew Johnson, opposed most of Stevens's plans. Stevens was up for the fight in August of 1866 during a Congressional speech. He proclaimed:

> You will remember in Egypt he sent frogs, locusts, murrain, lice, and finally demanded the firstborn of every one of the oppressors. Almost all these have been taken from us. We have been oppressed with taxes and debts, and he has sent us worse than lice and has afflicted us with Andrew Johnson.

It was Stevens who proposed the resolution for the impeachment of Johnson in 1868. Every Republican voted in favor of the measure, and Stevens made it a point to put members of both the House and Senate on notice relative to their ultimate decision on the matter. After the articles of impeachment were adopted, he said, "Let me see the recreant who would vote to let such a criminal escape. Point me to one who would dare do it, and I will show you one who would dare the infamy of posterity."

That man turned out to be a Republican Senator Edmund Ross from Kansas who found Johnson to be not guilty, and as a result, the president's impeachment failed by one slender vote. Rather than daring the infamy of posterity, Ross was hailed for his stand and vote in John F. Kennedy's *Profiles in Courage*.

While Stevens failed in his efforts to impeach the President, he was largely successful in having his policies adopted in terms of the Reconstruction of the South. In terms of historical judgment, Reconstruction is largely viewed as having failed. Historians differ as to the reasons for this outcome, and that remains a matter of controversy to this day.

Formal notice of the impeachment of Andrew Johnson, by the House Committee, Thaddeus Stevesn and John A. Bingham, at the bar of the Senate, Washington, D.C., on February 25, 1868.

The tomb of a man that would not accept slavery in the United States.

Three months after the acquittal of Johnson on August 11, 1868, Thaddeus Stevens died in Washington. He was 76 years of age. His coffin lay in state in the Capitol Rotunda, attended by a black honor guard. His funeral in Lancaster was attended by over 20,000 people, half of which were African Americans. He decided to be buried in the Shreiner Cemetery because it would accept people without regard to race. Stevens composed the inscription on his headstone. It reads:

> I repose in this quiet and secluded spot, not from
> any natural preference for solitude, but finding other
> cemeteries limited as to race, by charter rules. I have
> chosen this that I might illustrate in my death the
> principles which I advocated through a long life,
> equality of man before his Creator.

In death, Stevens attempted to carry on the causes he worked for during his life. He left $50,000 to establish the Stevens School. The school provided refuge and education to homeless orphans. The students were admitted without regard to their race or the religion of their parents. The school is now the Thaddeus Stevens College of Technology, and its goal remains to provide the underprivileged with opportunities they would otherwise be denied.

If You Go:

In *Keystone Tombstones Volume One,* we identified several sites worth visiting in Lancaster. We would urge you to review chapters 2, 21, and 24 in that publication, which covers the careers of President James Buchanan, the Pennsylvania patriot Thomas Mifflin, and Major General John Fulton Reynolds.

21.

GENERAL JOHN SUTTER
"After the Gold Rush"

County: Lancaster • Town: Lititz
Buried at Moravian Cemetery
212 East Main Street

On January 24, 1848, a man by the name of James Marshall was working on enlarging the tailrace of a sawmill to improve its efficiency. Marshall noticed flecks of metal that glittered in the stream. He gathered a few ounces so they could be chemically tested. The tests confirmed that Marshall had discovered gold. Ironically the discovery would lead to the California Gold Rush and result in the financial ruin of the man who owned the mill. His name was John Sutter.

Sutter was born on February 28, 1803, in Baden, Germany. When he was a young man, he tried his hand at several professions, including working as a clerk and serving as an apprentice in the publishing business. While working as a clerk, he met the woman who would become his wife. The Sutters were married on October 24, 1826, when he was 23 years old, and his bride was 21. Over the next five years, the Sutters produced four children: three sons and a daughter.

Sutter went into business for himself, but soon he was deep in debt. He had heard stories of the tremendous opportunities that existed in America and decided that it offered the opportunity for a fresh start. In 1834 he sold his business to his mother-in-law and headed for the New World. Mrs. Sutter was left behind to care for the children. Sutter was 31 when he arrived in America, and he decided his best prospects for success were in the West, so he settled in Missouri and began working as a trader. He managed a store in the area of what is now Kansas City. In 1838

General John Sutter

he joined a group of traders and headed to Vancouver. That same year, Sutter wanted to push on to California, but he decided against it when he received reports of severe winter storms and attacks by hostile Indians.

In July of 1839, Sutter landed at Monterey in California. He then gained permission from Governor Alvarado to explore the area along the Sacramento River. He agreed that if he found land suitable for a settlement, he would stay for one year before filing a claim for a grant of the property. Sutter then sold the goods he had brought with him and purchased three small ships that could be used to explore the river. On August 12, 1839, he landed in the vicinity of what is now 28th Street in Sacramento. It was here that he decided to build his settlement.

Under Sutter's leadership, the settlement prospered. On September 1, 1840, Sutter filed his claim on the land. The claim was approved, and Sutter was awarded about 48,000 acres of land. He named the area New Helvetia. He was also appointed judge for the area, and it was his responsibility to maintain law and order.

In the summer of 1841, Sutter began the construction of a large fort. The fort was completed in 1844, and the compound covered 75,000 square feet. Located within its walls were shops, a bakery, a flour mill, a distillery, and a blanket factory. Sutter minted tin coins that could be used within the community to purchase goods at any of the shops in the

James Marshall at Sutter's Mill, circa 1850. Source: Library of Congress, Prints &
Photographs Division, [LC-USZ62-137164].

fort. In 1841 Sutter also purchased Fort Ross, which was an unprofitable Russian fort located near Fort Sutter.

In 1846 war broke out between the United States and Mexico. It was Sutter's view that the Americans would emerge victoriously, so he raised the American flag over his fort and took an oath of allegiance to the United States. He allowed United States troops to be stationed at Fort Sutter at his own expense. The United States never reimbursed him for the funds he spent to support these troops.

Things were going very well for Sutter until gold was discovered at his sawmill. The discovery took place in late January 1848. By May, more than 4,000 prospectors were working around the mill. Within twelve months, the territory's population grew from 14,000 to over 100,000. Those who worked for Sutter now deserted him to seek their fortunes. The economic balance in Sutter's little community was destroyed, and he suffered huge losses. His lands were overrun by squatters who stole horses and cattle from the herds Sutter had built. In the summer of 1848, Sutter moved to Hock Farm on the Feather River, a piece of his property that had not been invaded by squatters. In 1850 his wife and children, who he had not seen in sixteen years, joined him at Hock Farm.

Even though Sutter had suffered significant financial losses, he was still very much respected in California. In 1849 he served as a member at the State Constitutional Convention. In 1853 he became a major general in the California State Militia.

The squatters who had settled around Fort Sutter disputed Sutter's claim to the land. Sutter, however, had already sold many lots throughout the disputed area. The case made it to the United States Supreme Court. In 1864 the Court upheld the legitimacy of the original grant. However, it denied Sutter's claim to lands he obtained after the initial grant. Sutter found that he could not give clear title to many who had purchased lots from him. He mortgaged Hock Farm and all but drained his remaining funds to meet his obligations.

At this point, Sutter decided to move east. Sutter's son, John Jr., had married a woman in Mexico. The marriage produced a son and two daughters. When the marriage failed, John Jr., who was unable to get a divorce, deserted his family. The three children became wards of their grandparents, and they accompanied Sutter and his wife on their trip east.

When Sutter arrived in the east, he enrolled the children in boarding schools, and he and his wife lived in various hotels for five years. The Sutters were living off a small pension from the state of California. During the winter months, they lived in Washington, D.C., where Sutter repeatedly petitioned Congress for reimbursement for the lands he had lost. Among the places they lived in the winter months was Pennsylvania. During one of these visits, they stayed at the Springs Hotel in Lititz, Pennsylvania. Sutter was impressed with the schools in the area, and he and his wife decided to make Lititz their home. Sutter bought a piece of land and built a home in the small town. He enrolled his grandchildren in local schools.

Sutter continued to travel to Washington to press his claim for reimbursement. In 1880 he was advised that his prospects relative to his claim looked positive. However, it was an election year, and Congress adjourned early, leaving many bills to die, including Sutter's petition.

This tombstone marks the grave site of General John Sutter.

Sutter was in his hotel room, writing a letter to his wife about this most recent setback, when he died on June 18, 1880.

Sutter's body was returned to Lititz for burial. The Moravian Brethren permitted Sutter's family to have him buried in their cemetery. This was an exception to their tradition that only church members be permitted to be buried there. When Mrs. Sutter passed away seven months later, they granted another exception, and she was buried with her husband.

Sutter's Fort was pilfered and permitted to fall into ruin until all that remained was Sutter's home. The Native Sons of the American West purchased the property in 1890 and donated it to the state. Reconstruction of the land began in 1892, and, in 1947, Sutter Fort became part of the California State Park System. The fort serves as a learning center for California, and it contains a large collection of artifacts relating to the Gold Rush years.

If You Go:

Lititz is a charming little town. We strongly recommend a stop at the Bulls Head Public House located just off the public square at 14 East Main Street. The Bulls Head is a traditional British Pub with 14 rotating taps and over 70 different bottled beer choices. We had lunch there, and the food was great and reasonably priced, and the service was fast and friendly. It's worth a visit.

The Springs Hotel, where Sutter stayed on his visit to Lititz, is now known as the General Sutter Inn. The Inn is located right next to the Bulls Head Public House and offers fine dining and casual fare. Weather permitting, you can choose to dine on the outdoor patio. The Inn is located across the street from the home Sutter built in Lititz.

Here's the General Sutter Inn in Lititz where we had a pint and enjoyed the company of our fellow patrons.

22.

CHARLES WILLIAM TATE

"Tuskegee Airman"

County: Allegheny • Town: Bridgeville
Buried at National Cemetery of the Alleghenies
1158 Morgan Road

Charles William Tate of Pittsburgh was a true American hero. His heroism had many facets, considering the role he played in the Army Air Corps during World War II and in black history. Charles William Tate was a Tuskegee Airman. The story of the Tuskegee Airmen is one of defying the odds, overcoming racism, and performing superbly in combat. They fought two wars—one against Nazi Germany and another against segregation at home and in the military.

Before the Tuskegee Airmen, no African American had become a U.S. military pilot. The U.S. Army Air Corps did not employ African Americans in any role. In 1940, President Roosevelt ordered the Air Corps to form an all-black flying unit. As a result, the army created the 99th Pursuit Squadron and opened a new training base at the Tuskegee Institute in central Alabama to develop the pilots needed for the new squadron.

The budding program got a publicity boost in March 1941 when First Lady Eleanor Roosevelt visited Tuskegee and was invited to take a ride by Charles "Chief" Anderson, head of the program. Over objections of the Secret Service agents, Mrs. Roosevelt accepted. One of the agents was so upset he called the president who replied: "Well, if she wants to do it, there's nothing we can do to stop her." Chief Anderson took off with Mrs. Roosevelt in the back seat of a Piper J-3 Cub and flew her around for half an hour.

Tuskegee Airmen of World War II

Progress was shown in 1941 as the first thirteen pilot candidates entered training. It wasn't until September 2 that Captain Benjamin Davis became the first African American to solo an aircraft as a U.S. Army Air Corps Officer. He would eventually become the U.S. Air Force's first black general in 1954. Under Davis's leadership, the 99th Pursuit Squadron added personnel and trained before finally being sent to North Africa in the spring of 1943.

Charles Tate left Oliver High School in Pittsburgh in 1942 and made his way into history by being one of the fighter squadron pilots who fought with Davis and the 99th Pursuit Squadron. Tate completed 99 missions and earned a commission of second lieutenant. His bravery earned him the Distinguished Flying Cross and four Oak Leaf Clusters. Oak Leaf Clusters are awarded for the subsequent award of the same decoration. The 99th was considered ready for combat duty and shipped out for North Africa in April 1943. They first saw combat on June 2, 1943, when they attacked the small strategic Italian island of Pantelleria in the Mediterranean Sea. They then saw action in Sicily and Italy before being deploys as bomber escorts in Europe, where they were particularly successful in their missions. When the pilots painted the tails of their P-47s red, the nickname "Red Tails" was coined. Bomber crews applied a more effusive "Red Tail Angels" sobriquet. The combat record of the Tuskegee Airmen speaks for itself:

450 Airmen, including pilots, bombardiers, and navigators served in combat in the European Theater of Operations, North Africa, and the Mediterranean.

66 of the Tuskegee aviators died in combat.

33 Tuskegee Airmen became prisoners of war.

They flew 15,533 sorties between May 1943 and June 1945.

They destroyed 251 enemy aircraft.

They sank a German destroyer using only their machine guns.

They won more than 850 medals, including 150 Distinguished Flying Crosses, eight Purple Hearts, fourteen Bronze Stars, 744 Air Medals and Clusters, and three Distinguished Unit Citations.

These achievements, together with the men and women who supported them on the ground, paved the way for full integration of the U.S. military. On July 26, 1948, President Truman issued Executive Order #9981 desegregating the Armed Forces.

And as if all that wasn't enough, Charles Tate re-enlisted and served as a captain during the Korean War. When he returned from Korea, he built a career in the U.S. Postal Service, rising to supervisor in the North Side Station before becoming the manager of the Homewood Station in Pittsburgh.

Charles William Tate died on November 18, 2005, in Pittsburgh at the age of 83. He is buried in the National Cemetery of the Alleghenies in Bridgeville, Pennsylvania.

In 1998, Motor Field, where the airmen trained, was declared the Tuskegee Airmen National Historic Site to commemorate the heroic actions of the Tuskegee Airmen during World War II. In March of 2007, the Tuskegee Airmen were awarded the Congressional Gold Medal, the most prestigious honor presented by the United States Congress.

The grave of one of Pittsburgh's Tuskegee Airmen.

In 1995, a film based on the exploits of the unit was broadcast on HBO. The movie *The Tuskegee Airmen* had a star-studded cast including Laurence Fishburne, Andre Braugher, Cuba Gooding, and John Lithgow and won an Emmy and the 1996 Peabody Award. Fishburne was nominated for a Golden Globe.

A more recent movie, *Red Tails*, released in early 2012, is also about the Tuskegee Airmen. The movie also starred Cuba Gooding and was produced by George Lucas.

A memorial honoring the Tuskegee Airmen was recently erected at Sewickley Cemetery near Pittsburgh.

If You Go:

Not far from the National Cemetery of the Alleghenies is Mount Lebanon Cemetery, where two recipients of the Congressional Medal of Honor are buried. Casper Carlisle served as a private in the Civil War. He served with the Pennsylvania Light Artillery and was awarded his Medal of Honor for his bravery on the second day of the Battle of Gettysburg

(July 2, 1863) when he "saved a gun from his battery under heavy musket fire" in the Peach Orchard.

William David Morgan served as a Marine corporal in Vietnam and was awarded the Medal of Honor for his bravery at the Vandergrift Combat Base in Quang Tri Province, Republic of Vietnam, on February 25, 1969. He was killed by enemy fire while trying to rescue two wounded Marines. His actions resulted in saving the lives of two fellow Marines. His medal was awarded to his family by President Richard Nixon in August 1970.

23.

GEORGE TAYLOR

"An Indentured Servant Who Became a Founding Father"

County: Northampton • Town: Easton
Buried at Easton Cemetery
401 North 7th Street

George Taylor was a signer of the Declaration of Independence as a representative of Pennsylvania. He was born in Ireland in 1716. As a young man, he wanted to come to America but couldn't pay his passage, so he became an indentured servant to Samuel Savage, who ran an iron foundry outside Philadelphia. He arrived in 1736 and started as a laborer, but when Savage discovered that Taylor had a certain degree of education, he made him a clerk in his foundry. In 1742, Savage died, and George married his widow, Ann, and took over the iron business. He and Ann would have two children.

He also had five children with his housekeeper Naomi Smith with whom he would carry on an affair for years.

He served in the provincial assembly from 1764 to 1769 and then was reelected in 1775. When problems with Britain surfaced, he immediately spoke out in favor of independence. In July 1775, as colonial forces prepared for war, he was commissioned as a colonel in the Third Battalion of the Pennsylvania militia.

In 1776, the Continental Congress voted for independence on July 2 and adopted the Declaration of Independence on July 4. Before the vote for independence, five of Pennsylvania's delegates, all loyalists, were forced to resign. On July 20, Taylor was among the replacements appointed by the assembly. One of his first duties was to affix his signature

George Taylor

to the Declaration of Independence, which he did on August 2. Of the 56 signers, he was one of only eight who were foreign-born, the only one to have been indentured, and the only ironmaster. He was elected to the First Supreme Executive Council of Pennsylvania in 1777 but soon became ill and retired from public life.

After George Taylor resigned from public office, he continued to support the patriots. From 1777 to 1780, Taylor worked at his iron mills, making cannon balls for the Continental Army. In 1780, Taylor became ill again and decided to return to his home in Easton. He spent the rest of his life there. He died on February 23, 1781, at the age of sixty-five.

Taylor's body was originally buried at St. John's Lutheran Church in Easton. In 1854, a memorial was constructed in the Easton Cemetery for Taylor. In 1870, his body was moved to the site of his memorial and was buried directly in front of it.

If You Go:

Also, in Easton Cemetery are the graves of Theophilus Rodenbough, a Congressional Medal of Honor recipient, and James Porter, the Founder of Lafayette College.

Rodenbough (Nov. 5, 1838 – Dec. 19, 1912) served in the Civil War and was awarded the Congressional Medal of Honor for his efforts at the Battle of Trevilian Station, Virginia, on June 11, 1864, where he was severely wounded. After he recovered, he lost his right arm at the Battle of Third Winchester on Sept 19, 1864. He also commanded the 2nd U.S. Cavalry during the Gettysburg Campaign.

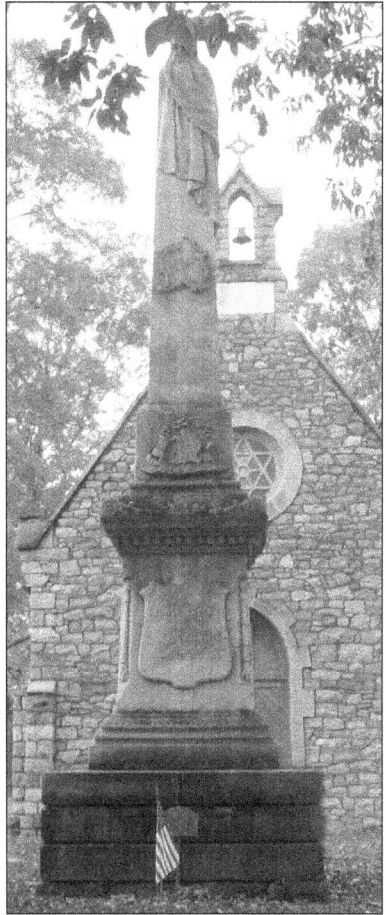

This is the tomb of George Taylor, a man who lived the American dream.

James Porter (Jan. 6, 1793 – Nov. 11, 1862) founded Lafayette College. He was a colonel in the Army during the War of 1812 and served as Secretary of War from 1843 to 1844 during the Tyler presidency.

24.

HARRY KENDALL THAW
"Murder at Madison Square Garden"

County: Allegheny • Town: Pittsburgh
Buried at Allegheny Cemetery
4734 Butler Street

On June 25, 1906, a man with the large mustache was seated in the privileged section of the dining theater on the roof of Madison Square Garden. He was there to see the opening of a new play called *Mam'zelle Champagne*. He was very well known in New York City and was the most distinguished architect of his time. He was sitting on the roof of a building he had designed. His name was Stanford White.

Another man was attending the play that night. Even though it was summer and quite warm, he wore a black overcoat. Earlier the hat check girl had attempted to check the coat, but her offer was refused. During the performance of a song titled "I Could Love a Million Girls," the man approached White's table. He reached into the overcoat and produced a pistol, and at point-blank range, shot White three times in the face. The architect fell to the floor, mortally wounded. The killer calmly moved toward the exit holding the murder weapon over his head. His name was Harry Thaw.

Thaw was born on February 12, 1871. His father, William Thaw, had made a fortune through both the coal and the railroad business. Even when he was very young, Thaw exhibited a violent nature. He did poorly at several private schools in Pittsburgh, and his teachers described him as a troublemaker. He gained admission, probably with the help of his father, to the University of Pittsburgh, where he planned to study law. A few years later, again using his social status, he was admitted to

Harry Kendall Thaw

Harvard. Thaw later said that his main field of study at Harvard was poker. He also did a lot of drinking and was finally expelled after he was arrested for chasing a cab driver through Cambridge with a shotgun.

It is believed that around this time, Thaw created the speedball, which involved the injection of morphine or heroin and cocaine.

After leaving Harvard, Thaw began hanging out in New York City. He made it a habit to inject himself with both morphine and cocaine. He enjoyed Broadway shows largely because of the chorus girls. It was during this time that he first met Stanford White, who also had a keen interest in chorus girls. One of these girls would play a key part in the lives of both men. Her name was Evelyn Nesbitt.

In the early 1900s, Nesbitt was one of the most sought-after models in New York. She appeared on the cover of *Vanity Fair*, *Cosmopolitan,* and *Harper's Bazaar*. She eventually tired of modeling and decided to move into the theater. In July of 1901, Nesbit joined the chorus line in a popular play called *Florodora*. It was here where Stanford White first noticed her. He was 47 years old and a known womanizer when he met Nesbit, who was 16 at the time.

White kept a loft apartment on West 24th Street. When Nesbitt first visited the apartment, she was impressed by the furnishings and fine paintings. She was given a glass of champagne and escorted upstairs to a studio that contained a red velvet swing. Nesbitt would later testify in court that White found sexual pleasure in pushing naked or very nearly naked young women in the swing. On a subsequent visit to the apartment, the two had dinner and multiple glasses of champagne. She was given a tour of the apartment and more champagne. She tried on a yellow satin kimono for White and then, in her own words, "passed out." When she awoke, she was in bed nearly naked, and White was beside her. When she entered the room, she was a virgin, but she did not leave as one. Having completed the conquest, White moved on and pursued other young women.

Around this time, Thaw became enamored with Nesbitt. White, who had warned other showgirls to stay away from Thaw, gave Nesbitt the same advice. At first, she heeded the warning and made it a point to avoid Thaw. Thaw took advantage of the situation when Nesbitt was admitted to a hospital due to appendicitis. He often visited showering her with gifts and praising her amazing talents. White had her moved to a sanatorium in upstate New York, but Thaw continued to visit her there.

Upon her release from the sanatorium, Thaw invited Nesbitt and her mother to visit Paris with him. While on this trip, Thaw proposed to Nesbitt, but she turned him down. While in Paris, he continued his practice of giving Nesbitt lavish gifts. Thaw also continued to ask her to marry him, and she confessed that White had taken her virginity, and therefore she wasn't worthy of marrying Thaw. The news built up the hatred Thaw already had regarding White. After he sent Nesbitt's

Evelyn Nesbitt

mother back to New York, he took the daughter to an isolated castle in Germany. It was here that Thaw forced himself sexually on Nesbitt and began beating her repeatedly with a dog whip. Finally, she convinced Thaw to return to New York.

Back in New York, Thaw continued in his pursuit to marry Nesbitt. He also harassed her about her relationship with White. Thaw began referring to White as "the beast." Thaw's mother went to see Nesbitt and urged her to marry her son. Nesbitt gave in and married Thaw, who seemed to lose interest in her after they became man and wife. At the same time, Thaw's obsession with White seemed to grow. Nesbitt later recalled that on a voyage to Europe, Thaw tied her to a bed and began beating her to force her to confess to every sexual act she had engaged in with White.

As detailed earlier in this chapter, Thaw eventually got his revenge regarding White. At the time of the shooting, witnesses said they heard Thaw say, "You ruined my life." Others reported that he said, "You ruined my wife." Whatever was said after the shooting, Thaw walked to the elevator where Nesbitt was waiting, and when she saw the gun in his hand, she exclaimed, "Oh Harry, what have you done?"

Thaw was arrested, charged with murder, and placed in the Tombs Prison. His prison life was far from ordinary. He didn't eat prison food; instead, his meals were catered by Delmonico's then one of New York's finest restaurants. He also had whiskey brought to him and was permitted to have visitors day and night. Meanwhile, his mother was assembling a defense team that would be led by Delphin Delmas, known as one of the finest defense attorneys in the country. The district attorney at the time was William Travers Jerome, who had declared Thaw a fiend and stated, "No matter how rich a man is, he cannot get away with murder."

It would take six months for what the press was calling "The Trial of the Century" to begin. The trial would last for seven months. The prosecution attempted to make the case that Thaw had committed premeditated murder. The defense claimed that Thaw was insane and that he had murdered White after being directed to do so by the spirits of the dead. The defense had doctors testify that, in their opinion, Thaw was insane. The defense even produced a medium who claimed that during a séance, a spirit spoke through her and confessed that it had forced Thaw to kill White. Nesbitt also testified, providing details on her seduction by White and of their sexual relations. Thaw's mother had convinced Nesbitt to testify by promising her a divorce and payment of one million dollars. After the trial, she got the divorce but not one cent of the money.

The jury was unable to return a verdict; seven jurors believed Thaw was guilty, but the other five judged him to be insane. Nine months later, Thaw was retried, and this jury found him not guilty by reason of insanity. The judge ordered that Thaw be placed in an asylum. Thaw made the trip to the asylum in a private train car loaded with friends. On the way, they drank whiskey and champagne and enjoyed a meal. Nesbitt did not accompany her husband on the trip. In 1913 Thaw walked out of the asylum and was driven to Canada. He was arrested in Canada and deported back to the United States, where, in 1915, a judge found him to be sane and ordered his release.

In 1916, Thaw was accused of sexually assaulting and beating Fred Gump, a high school student. After he was indicted, he left New York and went to Philadelphia. When he was found in Philadelphia, he had slashed his own throat, but the wound had not killed him. He was once again found to be insane and returned to an asylum. Seven years later, he was again declared sane and released.

After his release in 1924, Thaw purchased a home in Clearbrook, Virginia. His neighbors viewed him as being eccentric, but he managed to stay out of trouble with the law. He spent the rest of his life traveling to various locations around the world, and attractive young girls generally accompanied him. On February 22, 1947, while in Miami, Thaw died as a result of a heart attack; he was 76 years old. In his will, he left $10,000 to Evelyn Nesbitt, an amount that represented less than 1 percent of his wealth. Thaw's body was returned to Pittsburgh and was buried in Allegheny Cemetery.

While Thaw was in the asylum, Nesbitt gave birth to a son who she named Russell Thaw. Thaw, however, denied that the child was his. Without Thaw's financial support, Nesbitt was forced to return to the

Here is the family plot where the notorious Harry Thaw was laid to rest.

vaudeville stage. Despite another short marriage to a man named Jack Clifford, she was always billed as Mrs. Harry K. Thaw. Nesbitt moved to Northfield, New Jersey, where she battled an addiction to morphine and alcoholism. In 1955 she was a technical advisor for the movie *The Girl in the Red Velvet Swing*. The movie was a highly fictionalized story of the famous love triangle between her, Thaw, and White. The 1975 novel and later the film *Ragtime* also tell the story of the three lovers. Late in life, she declared that Stanford White was the only man she ever loved. She died in 1967 at the age of 82 in a nursing home in Santa Monica, California.

If You Go:

See the "If You Go" section in the chapter on Stephen Foster.

25.

JOHN WANAMAKER
"A Business Pioneer"

County: Philadelphia • Town: Philadelphia
Buried at Saint James the Less Episcopal Churchyard
3227 West Clearfield Street

John Wanamaker is the founder of Wanamaker's Department Stores and a pioneer in marketing and advertising. He was born in Philadelphia on July 11, 1838. Not much is known about his early life except that his father and grandfather were brick makers, but young John took jobs at a bookstore and several clothing stores. In 1860 he married Mary Erringer Brown in Philadelphia, and they had six children.

John was unable to join the Army during the Civil War due to a persistent cough and ventured into business with his brother-in-law opening a men's clothing store in 1861 in Philadelphia. Business grew substantially based on his principle "one price and goods returnable." Soon he opened a second store on Chestnut Street and then published the first copyrighted advertisement by a retailer. In 1875 he purchased an abandoned railroad depot and converted it into a large store called "the Grand Depot." It is the first department store in Philadelphia.

He was an innovator and guaranteed the quality of his merchandise in writing. His store was the first with electrical illumination, the first with a telephone, and the first to have a restaurant inside. He invented the price tag and allowed his customers to return purchases for a cash refund. In 1878 he offered the first "white sale" with special prices on linens and other white products.

He gave his employers free medical care, education, recreational facilities, pensions, and profit-sharing plans before such benefits were

John Wanamaker

popular. He was, however, a fierce opponent of unionization and fired the first twelve union members he discovered in 1887 during an organizing drive by the Knights of Labor.

John Wanamaker opened his first New York store in 1896 and continued to expand his business abroad with Houses of Wanamaker in London and Paris. A large, grander store in Philadelphia was completed in 1910 on the site of the "Grand Depot," encompassing an entire block at the corner of 13th and Market Streets across from City Hall. The store housed a large pipe organ called the Wanamaker Grand Court Organ and was dedicated by President William Howard Taft. The organ is still in use today for daily recitals and all sorts of special event concerts. The store's Grand Court also housed the Wanamaker Eagle, a 2500-pound bronze eagle that became a famous meeting place.

After so much success in business, Wanamaker developed an interest in politics and gave $10,000 to the campaign of Benjamin Harrison in the 1888 presidential race. When Harrison won, despite receiving fewer popular votes than his opponent Grove Cleveland, he appointed John Wanamaker as United States Postmaster General. During his term as postmaster, he achieved many reforms, such as extending mail service to rural areas and establishing the first parcel-post system. He issued the first commemorative stamps at the World's Columbian Exposition

John Wanamaker's Grand Depot Store, Philadelphia, PA, circa 1880. Opened in 1876, John Wanamaker's massive Grand Depot sprawled over the site of the former Pennsylvania Railroad freight depot. One of the great innovators in American retailing, Wanamaker introduced a number of innovations in this store. The Grand Depot was the first American department store to have electrical illumination (1878), telephone service (1879), pneumatic tubes to transport cash and documents (1880), and elevator service (1884).

Thomas Nast, ca. 1888. "$10,000 compliments of Pious John to help carry Indiana."
Nash suggest that department-store magnate "Pious John" Wanamaker gave away some of
his fortune to support the campaign of candidate Benjamin Harrison, who is wearing the
toolarge hat of his grandfather, President William Henry Harrison.

in Chicago in 1893. He believed the stamps, which commemorated Columbus's discovery of the New World, would generate revenue. Many in Congress were critical of the idea and thought it an unnecessary expense. Wanamaker was proven right when more than two billion stamps were sold at a value of forty million dollars. He also instituted the practice of sorting mail on a moving train to improve delivery time.

Wanamaker ran for the Republican nomination for the United States Senate in 1896 but lost to Boise Penrose. He then sought for the gubernatorial nomination in 1898 but lost again this time to William Stone.

This mausoleum houses the remains of the innovative store owner John Wanamaker.

Throughout his life, Wanamaker was a devout Presbyterian and worked for many years with the Bethany Sunday School and founded several Presbyterian churches. He was also able to maintain ties with the YMCA during his career and helped with the development of YMCA buildings all over the world.

John Wanamaker died in his home in Philadelphia on December 12, 1922. Thomas Edison, a close friend, was a pallbearer at his funeral. He is commemorated by a statue in front of Philadelphia's City Hall and buried in a large tower in the St. James the Less Episcopal Churchyard in Philadelphia. We were denied entrance into the tower by a caretaker who commented on not offending the family by allowing us to see inside.

If You Go:

Also buried at St. James the Less Episcopal Churchyard is Robert Morris Jr., the grandson of the Revolutionary War Patriot and Declaration of Independence signer, Robert Morris. He was a Union Civil War officer captured at the Battle of Brandy Station, Virginia, on June 9, 1863. He was imprisoned at the infamous Libby Prison, where he died on August 13, 1863.

The cemetery also contains the grave of Civil War Congressional Medal of Honor recipient Anthony Taylor, who enlisted as a private and was mustered out as a captain. He was awarded his Medal of Honor as a lieutenant for his bravery at the Battle of Chickamauga, Georgia, on September 20, 1863.

Also buried there is Benjamin Chew Tilghman, who served as an officer in the Civil War, was wounded at Chancellorsville, and upon recovery accepted the role of colonel and commander of the 3rd United States Colored Troops. After the war, he became famous for a variety of inventions, including the process of sandblasting.

Nearby St. James the Less at St. Timothy's Episcopal Church Cemetery in Roxborough section of Philadelphia is the grave of Orlando Henderson Petty. Petty was awarded the Congressional Medal of Honor for his "extraordinary heroism" in the Battle of Belleau Wood, France. He was also awarded the Distinguished Service Cross and the Croix de Guerre with palm from France and the Croce di Guerre from Italy.

26.

DICK WINTERS
AND
JOE TOYE

"Band of Brothers"

Counties: Lancaster and Berks • Towns: Ephrata and Laureldale
Winters is buried at Bergstrasse Cemetery
9 Hahnstown Rd
Toye is buried at Gethsemane Cemetery
3139 Kutztown Rd

At a time when the world needed heroes, Dick Winters and Joe Toye served in a company of heroes. Their heroics were chronicled first in a book by famous historian Stephen Ambrose and then in an HBO miniseries of the same title: *Band of Brothers.*

The story of Dick Winters begins and ends in Ephrata, Pennsylvania. He was born there on January 21, 1918, and moved to Lancaster at the age of eight. He was a reserved, hard-working boy who graduated from Lancaster Boys High School in 1937 and studied economics at Franklin and Marshall College, where he graduated in 1941.

Winters enlisted in the Army for what he thought would be one year in August 1941, months before Pearl Harbor. He was disillusioned by what he was experiencing in training camp, and after Pearl Harbor, he took the opportunity to attend Officer Candidate School. He graduated from OCS at Fort Benning, Georgia, on July 2, 1942. He realized then that he was going to war, and he wanted to serve with the best, so he volunteered for the paratroopers and was assigned to Company E (known as Easy Company), 2nd Battalion, 506th Parachute Infantry Regiment (PIR). The 506th was an experiment in that it was the first to be trained

Dick Winters

as a unit. The training was very tough. Only 148 officers completed the training out of 500 who volunteered. Out of 5300 enlisted men, only 1800 finished. In June 1943, the 506 PIR became attached to the 101st Airborne.

The first combat for Winters and Easy Company was Operation Overlord, the D-Day Invasion of France. They were dropped behind enemy lines just after midnight on June 6, 1944. The company commander was killed before he ever jumped, and Winters was suddenly the man in charge. Winters survived the jump, but because of withering anti-aircraft fire from below, they were dropped off-target, and Winters had lost his weapon and contact with his men. Somehow, he managed to keep his cool, survive through the night, meet up with thirteen other members of Easy Company (including Joe Toye), battle a few patrols, and regroup with the main force.

Later that day, he and his thirteen members of Easy Co. were ordered to take out a German artillery bunker that was raining fire on Utah Beach, where Allied forces were coming ashore. The bunker was defended by fifty German troops and contained four 150 mm heavy guns. Winters divided his squad into two groups. One group laid down covering fire with machine guns while he and a second group attacked the guns one at a time using grenades and TNT to disable them. Winters was shot in the leg, but it didn't stop him from continuing to lead the assault. This action has been called the Brécourt Manor Assault and is still taught at West Point as a textbook case of an assault on a fixed position. As a result of the assault that Winters planned, he and his men saved countless lives. Winters was awarded the Distinguished Service Cross, a promotion to captain, and a place in American military lore all in his first combat maneuver. Later that afternoon, one of the men found a jug of cider and passed it around. When it came to Winters, he shocked his men by taking a long pull. It was the first alcohol he ever tasted. He thought it might calm him down, he later explained. That night before lying down for some much-needed sleep, he made a promise to himself: If he lived through the war, he was going to find an isolated farm somewhere and spend the rest of his life in peace and quiet.

After helping capture the Nazi-infested town of Carentan, Winters and his men were chosen for Operation Market Garden in Holland in September 1944. This involved parachuting deep behind enemy lines, being surrounded, and stopping an attack on the 2nd Battalion's flank. While on patrol, they encountered a large group of Germans at a crossroads where the enemy were firing on American troops. Winters led his thirty-five men in an attack on three hundred Germans and routed them. This experience further sealed the bond between Winters and his men. After this, on October 9, Winters became the battalion executive officer, which was normally held by a major, but Winters filled it while a captain.

As if they hadn't done enough, in December, the 101st Airborne was moved by truck to Bastogne, Belgium, to defend against a German counter-offensive in what became known as the Battle of the Bulge. They were surrounded but held off elite German forces for a week of non-stop fighting until the U.S. Third Army broke through the German lines and, as the press reported, "rescued" them. No member of the 101st has ever agreed that they needed to be rescued.

Even after being relieved at Bastogne, Winters and his men weren't done. Easy Company led an attack on the town of Foy a few days later. The attack was successful, and on March 8, 1945, Winters was promoted to major. Shortly after, he was made acting battalion commander.

In May, Easy Co. was ordered to capture Berchtesgaden and Hitler's summer home, The Eagle's Nest. They were still there when the war ended on May 8, 1945.

On the way to Berchtesgaden, the company discovered a Nazi concentration camp that was part of the Dachau complex. They saw thousands of prisoners starving in striped pajamas and hundreds of corpses that were little more than skeletons. Winters wrote in his log: "the memory of starved, dazed men who dropped their eyes and heads when we looked at them through the chain-linked fence, in the same manner that a beaten, mistreated dog would cringe, leave feelings that cannot be described and will never be forgotten. The impact of seeing those people behind that fence left me saying, only to myself, 'Now I know why I am here.'"

Winters remained in Europe until the fall of 1945. On November 29, he arrived at Ft. Indiantown Gap, Pennsylvania. In 1948, he met and married his wife, Ethel Estoppey. In 1951 they bought a farm in Fredericksburg, Pennsylvania, where they settled and raised two children. In 1972, he started his own animal feed business and moved to Hershey, Pennsylvania. He retired in 1997.

Winters led the quiet life he promised himself until he suddenly found himself a celebrity. He met Stephen Ambrose in 1988, and in 1992, Ambrose published *Band of Brothers,* which chronicled the experiences of Easy Company. In 2001, it was turned into an HBO miniseries directed by Steven Spielberg and Tom Hanks. English actor Damien Lewis portrayed Winters. The miniseries won six Emmy Awards, a Golden Globe, an American Film Institute Award, and a Peabody Award.

Winters published his memoir in 2006 with co-writer Colonel Cole Kingseed. It's titled *Beyond Band of Brothers: The War Memoirs of Major Dick Winters*. In 2009, Franklin Marshall College conferred an Honorary Doctorate upon Winters.

Winters died at an assisted living facility in Campbelltown, Pennsylvania, on January 2, 2011. He had had Parkinson's disease for several years. He is buried in a very modest grave in Bergstrasse Lutheran Church cemetery in Ephrata, Pennsylvania.

Joseph D. Toye was born in Hughestown, Luzerne County, on March 14, 1919. His father, Peter, was a coal miner. Joe enlisted in the Army on December 11, 1941, in Wilks-Barre, Pennsylvania, four days after Pearl Harbor. He volunteered for the paratroopers after basic training and was stationed at Camp Toccoa, Georgia, and assigned to Easy Company. He completed the rigorous training and was one of the most respected men in the company. He made his first combat jump on D-Day in France and was one of the few who met up with Winters shortly after hitting the ground. He suffered a severe hand injury on the jump. He helped take out a German patrol on their way to the town of St. Come-du-Monte. He was one of the thirteen with Winters when they took out the guns at Brécourt Manor, and for his valor that day, he was awarded the Silver Star, the third-highest combat decoration that can be awarded.

He was with Easy Company in Operation Market Garden, where, desperate for information about enemy forces, he left the squad, went out in no-man's land by himself, and brought back a live prisoner for interrogation.

On New Year's Day, 1945, the newly promoted Sergeant Toye was hit by shrapnel during a bombing by German planes just outside of Bastogne. This was his third wound; he had been hit in Normandy and again in Holland. He was evacuated to Bastogne for treatment. He could have been evacuated to a rear echelon hospital but asked to be returned to the front. When Major Winters suggested he take it easy for a few days, he answered, "I want to be with my buddies." Two days later, he lost his right leg in a heavy artillery barrage. His buddy, William Guarnere, also lost his right leg while trying to drag Sgt. Toye to safety. Shrapnel also hit Toye in the chest, stomach, and arms. The shrapnel in his chest was removed in two separate operations, taking it out from the back.

Joe Toye spent about nine months in hospitals and was finally discharged from an Army hospital in Atlantic City, New Jersey. He had been awarded

Joe Toye

This tombstone marks the grave of Dick Winters who was certainly one of the greatest in the "Greatest Generation."

Here is the modest grave of four-time Purple Heart recipient Joe Toye, a true hero of World War II.

four Purple Hearts, a Silver Star, and a Bronze Star. It wasn't easy for him to find work with his disability, but he finally found work with Bethlehem Steel in Reading as a drill bit grinder.

He was married twice, the first time while recovering in the hospital. He had three sons and one daughter and seven grandchildren.

Sergeant Joseph Toye died of cancer in Reading on September 3, 1995. Dick Winters delivered his eulogy: "Every man in Company E would tell you that when the chips were down in combat, he would like to have Sgt. Joe Toye protecting his flank," Winters said.

In the HBO miniseries, actor Kirk Acevedo portrayed Joe Toye. He is buried in a very modest grave in Gethsemane Cemetery in Laureldale, near Reading, Pennsylvania.

The Emmy-winning HBO miniseries *Band of Brothers* transformed Dick Winters and Joe Toye and all the men of Easy Company into cultural icons. They have become the embodiment of millions of American servicemen who marched off to war as ordinary men but achieved extraordinary things.

One person who was inspired by the story of Easy Company is Jordan Brown, a young central Pennsylvania student. He heard of an effort to erect a statue in St. Marie Du-Mont, Normandy, France, honoring all the men who served on D-Day. Jordan created olive green wristbands that are inscribed with the expression "Hang Tough" on it. Dick Winters was known for having used the expression often. The wristbands were distributed for a minimum donation of one dollar. Jordan's efforts attracted attention and gained steam, and as of March 2012, his mother reported that he raised over $92,000, and the statue was dedicated on June 6th, 2012. Jordan was in attendance.

If You Go:
We found a great place to eat and replenish our vital bodily fluids in West Reading. The 3rd and Spruce Café on 3rd Avenue had a great menu of food and drinks, a great atmosphere, terrific service, and an owner who liked our mission so much; he picked up the check. If you go there, be sure to use the restroom and be sure to look up and enjoy the unusual décor.

Also buried in Gethsemane Cemetery is four-time all-star third basemen George "Whitey" Kurowski. He played nine seasons (1941–1949) with the St. Louis Cardinals.

Another baseball great is buried a few miles away in Reiffton at the beautiful Forest Hills Memorial Park. Carl Furillo played right field for the Brooklyn Dodgers from 1946–1960. Nicknamed "The Reading Rifle" because of his strong arm, Furillo batted over .300 five times and won the 1953 batting title with a 344 average. He also recorded ten or

Here are the authors with the owner of the 3rd and Spruce Café in Reading. He liked us so much he picked up our tab for lunch.

more assists in nine consecutive seasons. He played in seven World Series, six of them against the Yankees, winning in 1955 and 1959 against the White Sox. He was one of the players featured in Roger Kahn's 1972 landmark book *Boys of Summer*. When Kahn found him while writing the book, he was installing elevators in the World Trade Center. Furillo died in 1989 of a heart attack at home in Stony Creek Mills, Pennsylvania, at the age of 66.

Charles Evans Cemetery is also in Reading and contains many historical figures and unusual graves. Some of the people buried there will be discussed in future volumes.

27.

MEDAL OF HONOR RECIPIENTS

"A nation reveals itself not only by the men it produces
but also, by the men it honors, the men it remembers."
—President John F. Kennedy

The Medal of Honor is the highest award for valor in action against an enemy force which can be bestowed upon an individual serving in the Armed Services of the United States—generally presented to its recipient by the President of the United States of America in the name of Congress. The deed performed must have been one of personal bravery or self-sacrifice so conspicuous as to clearly distinguish the individual above his comrades and must have involved risk of life. Incontestable proof of the performance of the service will be exacted, and each recommendation for the award of this decoration will be considered on the standard of extraordinary merit.

In *Keystone Tombstones Volume One*, we visited and memorialized fifteen of Pennsylvania's Medal of Honor recipients. The response from readers was extremely positive. In *Volume Two*, we once again visited Medal of Honor recipients everywhere we went and have included nineteen in this volume. Along the way, we discovered that Pennsylvania honors its Medal of Honor recipients in Soldier's Grove in Harrisburg. Located directly behind the Capitol, the park serves as a memorial to all Pennsylvanians who have served in the U.S. armed forces. Included within the ribbon-like bands that represent various conflicts are the names of each Medal of Honor recipient for that conflict from Pennsylvania. Pennsylvania is second only to New York in the number of Medal of Honor recipients.

On the following pages are pictures of graves or the markers in Soldier's Grove of the recipients we visited in our travels for *Volume Two*.

Alfred L. Pearson

Archibald H. Rowand

THEOPHILUS F RODENBOUGH
MEDAL OF HONOR
BRIG GEN 2 US CAVALRY
CIVIL WAR
NOV 5 1838   DEC 19 1912

ORLANDO HENDERSON PETTY
6/11/1918
BOISE DE BELLEAU FRANCE

WILLIAM D MORGAN
MEDAL OF HONOR
CPL US MARINE CORPS
VIETNAM
SEP 17 1947   FEB 25 1969

DEWITT CLINTON LEWIS
MEDAL OF HONOR
BVT LIEUT COL CO F
97 PA INFANTRY
CIVIL WAR
JUL 30 1822   JUN 28 1899

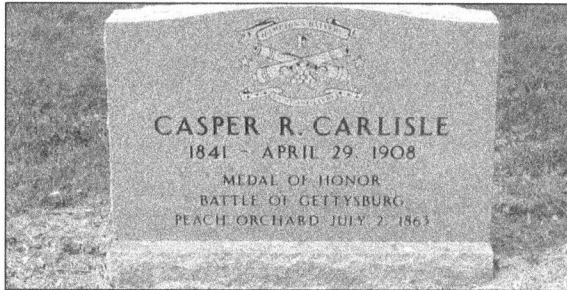

This is Soldier's Grove in Harrisburg a site that honors all of Pennsylvania's Medal of Honor recipients.

REUBEN S. SMALLEY
7/2/1863
ELK RIVER, TENNESSEE

GEORGE CRAWFORD PLATT
7/3/1863
FAIRFIELD, PENNSYLVANIA

CHARLES E. CAPEHART
7/4/1863
MONTEREY MOUNTAIN, PA

28.

UNUSUAL TOMBSTONES

Grave in Holy Cross Cemetery near Philadelphia.

The large monument is the only tombstone we have seen that has a skull on it.

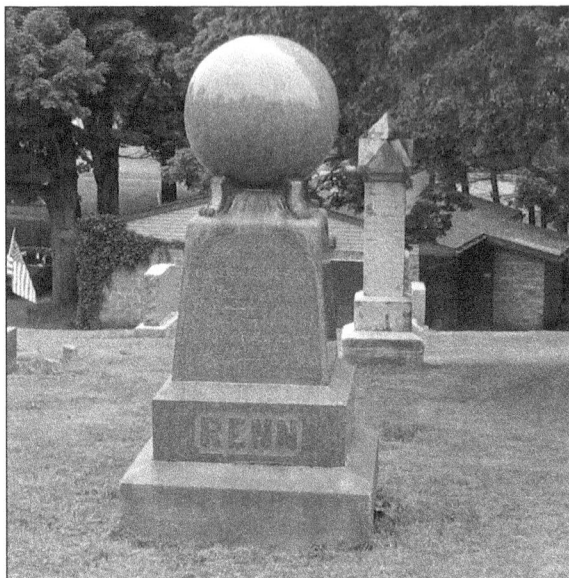

This grave is in Sunbury and we think this fellow was in a bowling league.

We found this grave at Calvary Cemetery in West Conshohocken.

A beautiful memorial in Lewisburg Cemetery.

For the life of us we don't know what this man was trying to get across.

We found this tombstone in
Montgomery Cemetery in
Norristown.

We found this tomb in Allegheny
Cemetery in Pittsburgh. It looks like
someone could live in there.

This tombstone is in Montgomery Cemetery in Norristown.

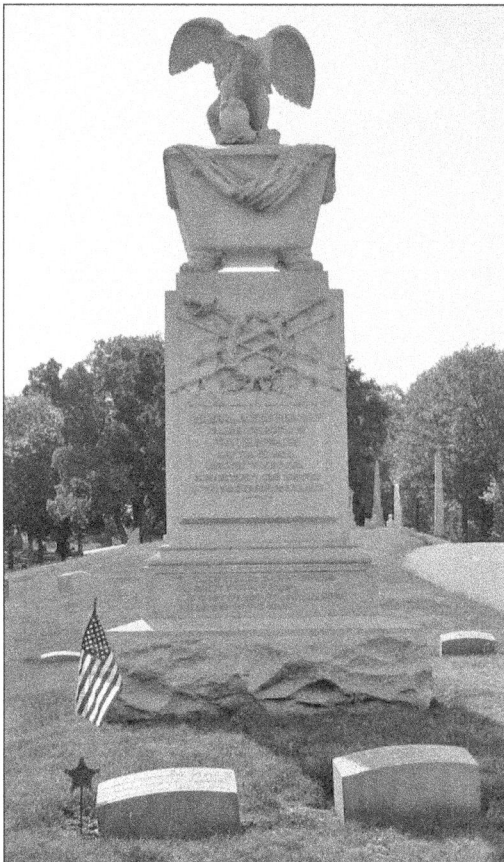

The man beneath this unusual grave was killed in the Civil War during the Battle of the Wilderness.

Another unusual grave we came upon in beautiful Allegheny Cemetery in Pittsburgh. You could spend all day in this cemetery and not see everything.

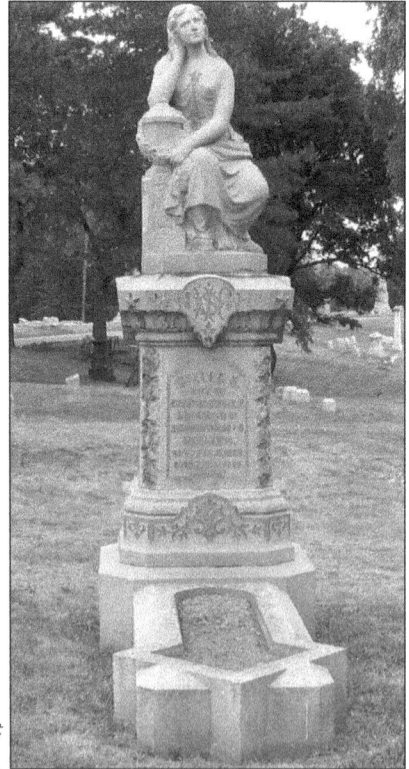

Another unusual grave we found at Allegheny Cemetery in Pittsburgh.

We wonder if this gentleman walked like an Egyptian.

This unusual grave is located in Evergreen Cemetery in Gettysburg.

213

We found this unusual grave in the Charles Evans Cemetery in Reading.

This grave is located in the Charles Evans Cemetery in Reading.

Just the paperboy on the corner.

This grave of a WWI soldier is located in Grandview Cemetery in Johnstown. The statue was sculpted in Europe from a picture of him and shipped to the United States.

*From Oakland's Cemetery in West
Chester.*

*Another unusual grave in the Charles
Evans Cemetery in Reading.*

SOURCES

Books, Magazines, Journals, Files:

Ambrose, Stephen E. *Band of Brothers: E Company, 506th Regiment, 101st Airborne from Normandy to Hitler's Eagle's Nest.* New York: Simon & Schuster, 2001.

Anastasia, George. *Blood and Honor: Inside the Scarfo Mob--The Mafia's Most Violent Family.* Philadelphia: Camino Books, 2003.

Archer, Jules. *The Plot to Seize the White House: The Shocking TRUE Story of the Conspiracy to Overthrow F.D.R.* New York: Skyhorse Publishing, 2005.

Bowen, Catherine Drinker. *Miracle at Philadelphia: The Story of the Constitutional Convention May to September 1787.* Boston, Massachusetts: Little, Brown & Company, 1966.

Brands, H. W. *The First American: The Life and Times of Benjamin Franklin.* New York: Doubleday, 2000.

Butler, Smedley D. *General Smedley Darlington Butler: The Letters of a Leatherneck, 1898-1931.* Santa Barbara, California: ABC-CLIO, 1992.

———. *War Is a Racket.* New York: Round Table Press, 1935.

Conlin, Joseph R. *The Morrow Book of Quotations in American History.* New York: William Morrow & Company, 1984.

Farrell, Joe & Joe Farley. *Keystone Tombstones Volume 1.* Mechanicsburg, Pennsylvania: Sunbury Press, 2011.

Jordan, David M. *Winfield Scott Hancock: A Soldier's Life.* Bloomington, Indiana: Indiana University Press, 1995.

Kahn, Roger. *The Boys of Summer.* New York: Harper Collins, 1972.

Kennedy, John F. *Profiles in Courage.* New York: Harper, 2003.

Kiernan, Denise & Joseph D'Agnese. *Signing Their Lives Away: The Fame and Misfortune of the Men Who Signed the Declaration of Independence.* Philadelphia: Quirk Books, 2008.

———. *Signing Their Rights Away: The Fame and Misfortune of the Men Who Signed the United States Constitution.* Philadelphia: Quirk Books, 2011.

Knorr, Lawrence K. *Gettysburg Eddie: The Story of Eddie Plank.* Mechanicsburg, Pennsylvania: Sunbury Press, 2018.

Langguth, A. J. *Patriots: The Men Who Started the American Revolution.* New York: Simon and Schuster, 1988.

Macht, Norman. *Connie Mack and the Early Years of Baseball*. Lincoln, Nebraska: University of Nebraska Press, 2007.

Maier, Pauline. *American Scripture: Making the Declaration of Independence*. New York: Alfred A. Knopf, Inc., 1997.

McPherson, James M. *Battle Cry of Freedom: The Civil War Era*. Oxford: Oxford University Press, 1988.

Meany, Tom. *Baseball's Greatest Pitchers*. New York: A. S. Barnes and Company, 1951.

Miller, Jr., Arthur P. & Marjorie L. Miller. *Pennsylvania Battlefields and Military Landmarks*. Mechanicsburg, Pennsylvania: Stackpole Books, 2000.

Millett, Allan R. & Peter Maslowski. *For the Common Defense: A Military History of the United States of America*. New York: The Free Press, 1984.

Meany, Tom. *Baseball's Greatest Pitchers*. New York: A. S. Barnes and Company, 1951.

Mudgett, Jeff. *Bloodstains*. Self-published, 2011.

Peterson, Robert W. *Only the Ball Was White: A History of Legendary Black Players and All-Black Professional Teams*. New York: Oxford University Press, 1992.

Shaara, Michael. *Killer Angels*. New York: Ballantine Books, 1996.

Westcott, Rich. *Winningest Pitchers: Baseball's 300-Game Winners*. Philadelphia: Temple University Press, 2002.

Winters, Dick & Cole C. Kingseed. *Beyond Band of Brothers: The War Memoirs of Major Dick Winters*. New York: Dutton Caliber, 2008.

Wood, Gordon S. *The Radicalism of the American Revolution*. New York: Vintage Books, 1993.

———. *The Americanization of Benjamin Franklin*. Oxford: Oxford University Press, 2009.

Zimniuch, Fran. *Richie Ashburn Remembered*. New York: Sports Publishing LLC, 2005.

Movies and Television Shows:

Band of Brothers (miniseries). Created by Tom Hanks and Steven Spielberg. New York: HBO, 2001.

Gettysburg. Directed by Ronald F. Maxwell. Atlanta: Turner Pictures, 1993.

Gods and Generals. Directed by Ronald F. Maxwell. Atlanta: Turner Pictures, 2003.

Ragtime. Directed by Miloš Forman. Los Angeles: Paramount Pictures, 1981.

Red Tails. Directed by Anthony Hemingway. Los Angeles: 20th Century Fox, 2012.

The Girl in the Red Velvet Swing. Directed by Richard Fleischer. Los Angeles: 20th Century Fox, 1955.

The Johnstown Flood. Directed by Charles Guggenheim. Johnstown, Pennsylvania: The Johnstown Flood Museum, 1989.

The Pittsburgh Kid. Directed by Jack Townley. Los Angeles: Republic Pictures, 1941.

The Tuskegee Airmen. Directed by Robert Markowitz. New York: HBO Pictures, 1995.

Online Resources:

Ancestry.com – Family tree information and vital records.

FamousAmericans.net – for information on many individuals.

FindaGrave.com – for burial information, vital statistics and obituaries.

Newspapers.com – Hundreds of newspaper articles were accessed—too numerous to mention here.

Philliesnation.com – Philadelphia Phillies information.

Press.uillinois.edu – University of Illinois Press.

TeachingAmericanHistory.com – for information on many individuals.

TheHistoryJunkie.com – for information on many individuals.

USHistory.org – for information on many individuals.

Wikipedia.com – for general historical information.

Other Resources:

Fred Rogers Center, Latrobe, Pennsylvania – Information about Fred Rogers.

Johnstown Flood Museum, Johnstown, Pennsylvania – Information about the Johnstown Flood.

INDEX

Congressional Medal of Honor Recipients

Cemeteries

Cities and Towns

Pubs and Restaurants

www.ingramcontent.com/pod-product-compliance
Lightning Source LLC
Chambersburg PA
CBHW021358090426

42742CB00009B/906